D0592499

CHANGING MY WORLD

CHANGES IN OUR WORLD

THE CHANGE BOOK

How Things Happen

Mikael Krogerus & Roman Tschäppeler

Translated by Jenny Piening

WITH ILLUSTRATIONS BY
PHILIP EARNHART AND DAG GRØDAL

W. W. Norton & Company
New York • London

For information about permission to reproduce selections from this book, write to
Permissions, W. W. Norton & Company, Inc., 500 Fifth Avenue, New York, NY 10110

For information about special discounts for bulk purchases, please contact
W. W. Norton Special Sales at specialsales@wwnorton.com or 800-233-4830

Manufacturing by Courier Westford
Production manager: Julia Druskin

Library of Congress Cataloging-in-Publication Data

Krogerus, Mikael.
[Welt erklärt in drei Strichen. English]
The change book : how things happen / Mikael Krogerus & Roman Tschäppeler ;
translated by Jenny Piening ; with illustrations by Philip Earnhart and Dag Grødal.
— First American edition.
pages cm
"The original edition was published in 2011 under the title Die Welt erklärt
in drei Strichen by Kein &Aber, Zurich."
Includes bibliographical references.
ISBN 978-0-393-24036-8 (hardcover)
1. Change. 2. Social change. 3. Change (Psychology) I. Tschäppeler, Roman.
II. Title.
BD373.K7613 2015
003—dc23

2014031055

W. W. Norton & Company, Inc., 500 Fifth Avenue, New York, N.Y. 10110
www.wwnorton.com
W. W. Norton & Company Ltd., Castle House, 75/76 Wells Street,
London W1T 3QT

1 2 3 4 5 6 7 8 9 0

CONTENTS

EXPLAINING MY WORLD

CHANGING MY WORLD

CHANGING OUR WORLD

APPENDIX

WHAT IT'S ABOUT

This book is about change—from the small and seemingly insignificant changes in our day-to-day lives to the big and almost incomprehensible changes in world history. And it is about the nagging feeling many of us have that we ought to be challenging the status quo. But if we want to change things we have to understand them first.

Why do we have less and less time? Why has everything become so complicated? Is democracy the right political system? Who governs the world? Why are we unfaithful? Why has air travel become so cheap?

For this book we talked to experts, studied theories and cross-examined existing knowledge. We wanted to understand, make sense of—and present—some of today's fundamental upheavals. The result is a visual travel guide through our time, a compilation of practical models, concrete theories and bold thought experiments that explain our world. Of course, the fifty-two theories in this book are only a selection. Some are more serious than others. And none of the theories are explored in depth: they are food for thought that we hope will whet your appetite to find out more.

This book is an attempt to present complex ideas succinctly and in layman's terms. You have to limit yourself to explain something. So don't expect academic tracts or state-of-the-art infographics. Instead, look forward to surprisingly simple explanations of our inexplicable world—and to having some of your preconceived ideas radically challenged.

WHY MODELS?

We tend to perceive things first in images, then in words. We remember pictures better than text and are more likely to recognize patterns in images than in sentences. Which is why science often attempts to explain highly complex ideas using simple formulae. But as we set out to write this book, we found that not every idea we wanted to explore had an existing model. So we collaborated with the Norwegian designer Dag Grødal, whose day job is to visualize the change processes of a big Scandinavian bank, and developed our own visual models. These models are illustrations of our time. They attempt to explain in images ideas that cannot be grasped in words.

In our quest for models to explain our world in terms of change, it soon became clear that we would have to revise our own concept of change. Contrary to what change management would have us believe, change does not imply a temporary transition from one state to another. The idea of *being* has to be replaced by the notion of *becoming*. This academic term describes the paradoxical simultaneity of stagnation and change.

INSTRUCTIONS FOR USE

Borrowing from the French philosopher Michel Foucault, we would like our book to be used as a kind of toolbox. The models are folding rules, screwdrivers, hammers, drills and spirit levels that you can use to measure, unscrew, modify and reassemble your world. You can open the box, take out individual sentences or models and use them as tools to break up your ideas of the world into their different components—including the ideas from which this book emerged.

There is nothing that can't be explained.

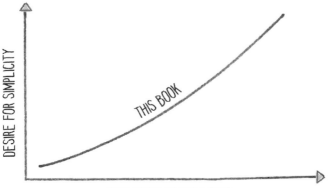

EXPLAINING OUR WORLD

HOW IT ALL BEGAN

LOOP QUANTUM COSMOLOGY
Our universe is part of a bigger entity,
in which universes with different laws
of nature continually expand and
contract, with no beginning and no end
(Martin Bojowald)

BIG BANG
The universe arose from
a quantum singularity
13.7 billion years ago
(Einstein, Guth)

STEADY STATE
The appearance of the
universe never changes, but
it expands and new matter is
continually created (Herman
Bondi)

FOR EXPERTS

We don't
understand

CLOCKWORK UNIVERSE
The universe is like a
mechanical system determined
by the laws of nature
(Pierre-Simon Laplace)

SOCIAL CONSTRUCTIVISM
Cosmology is an expression of
covert power relationships of
our social reality

SOLIPSISM
The universe is MY
invention

How the world came into being has always been a matter of heated
debate. Which version do you agree with?

OO COMPLEX

C. F. VON WEIZSÄCKER
Ur-alternatives:
Quantum-physical reality of the universe results from information-theoretical consequences of the subject-object dichotomy

STEPHEN HAWKING
Universe with imaginary time without a beginning or boundaries is a mathematical necessity from the yet-to-be-discovered "theory of everything"

ANTHROPIC PRINCIPLE
The universe developed in such a way that conscious life-forms capable of understanding the universe could come into being

JOHN WHEELER
"It from bit": matter is an epiphenomenon of information

FOR ALL

CREATION
God created heaven and earth (Old Testament)

MATRIX UNIVERSE
We are living within the computer simulation of a more advanced civilization

INDIAN COSMOLOGY
The universe is "uncreated," it moves in endless cycles (Buddhism)

KALEVALA
The universe was always there (Finnish mythology)

TOO SIMPLE

WHAT HAPPENS IF NOTHING HAPPENS ANYMORE?

"What is the engine of history?" There is a raft of theories that deal directly or indirectly with this question.

Thomas Hobbes believed in the survival instinct, Adam Smith in self-interest, Karl Marx in the class struggle. Georg Wilhelm Friedrich Hegel said the engine that led us from primeval tribal society through serfdom to democracy was the "struggle for recognition." According to his philosophy, historical development is about the recognition of the individual. History ends in a state without political contradictions in which the human desire for recognition is satisfied: in the liberal democratic state. (Karl Marx's approach was similar but the development he described had a different aim: a communist and classless society, which is not based on the principle of recognition but on redistribution.) Hegel believed the end of history had been reached in 1806 when Napoleon defeated Prussia in the Battle of Jena, which signified the triumph of the French Revolution over the aristocracy. Friedrich Nietzsche was also influenced by Hegel. He called a person who received recognition in the Hegelian sense "the last man": "Everybody wants the same, everybody is the same . . . whoever feels different goes voluntarily into a madhouse . . . 'We have invented happiness,' say the last men, and they blink." In the 1990s the American political scientist Francis Fukuyama seized the notion of the end of history and proclaimed that it had materialized with the end of the Cold War since only one system had survived: liberal capitalism. He was severely criticized. His critics called the terrorist attacks of September 11 "the end of the end of history." Fukuyama was refuted most convincingly by the fact that great powers such as Russia and China remained authoritarian states which have little in common with liberal democracy but still become ever richer thanks to capitalism.

Fukuyama defended his argument, pointing to the fact that even the recent financial crisis had not resulted in a fundamental change of the capitalist economic system and that even more recent revolutions like the uprisings in Arab countries were inspired by Western liberal values. In short: history is still at an end.

So, what next? Fukuyama predicted an age of boredom once history had ended. The terrible feeling that in a world without contradictions, in which everything is possible, nothing has value anymore. What are the possible consequences?

- History could start again. Or repeat itself.
- A return to nationalism, as the experience of a crisis-ridden Europe indicates.
- A renaissance of communism.
- A step toward a new world order.

"It is completely wrong to imagine that the [Arab] revolutionaries want the same liberal capitalism that exists in the West. They want more." *Slavoj Žižek*

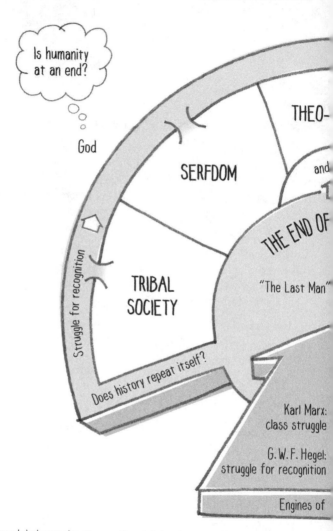

The model shows the stages of social development from the first tribes to democracy. What was the engine of this progress?

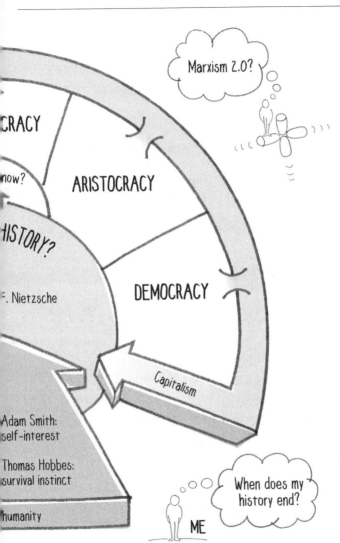

WHY X IS THE NEW Y

sincerity   smart → rich → poor ↔ middle class   Hitler
   ↓   Elvis ← Bin Laden → Che
irony   sexy   slim   pure   Guevara
   ↓
trans-fat   Genome → Gold Standard   Silver Euro   Martin Luther King
                                         subprime mortgage

security → freedom
        forgetting global unpaid jobs   The Cloud   DIY   Obama —
me   lying → normal ← green business   black ← vegan ←
 ↑   red   gay
we   Middle East ← Iraq → Iran   blue   bitch white
 ↓   pink
content → King   Dubai ← Beirut   gardening   Atheism
Denmark   Ginger
            Sealand   Kabul   AOL Prozac
Sweden → Los Angeles cause of divorce   Kanye
Kreuzkölln → Lower East Side   small   ← Facebook → Internet
Singapore → Switzerland   ↑
                               small   MTV New World Order
Futura → Helvetica   ↓
fisting → cuming on girl's face big thing ← Halal Food Chaos
Porno   TED → Harvard   ↑   ← Behavioral Economics
          visual note taking   decorating homes
Happy Days   Malbec Monday with water fountains
serial monogamy Religion   El Bulli Tuesday food Agamben
    ↓   ↑
polygamy   environmentalism Noma Sunday famine Tulum —

For this model, variations of the sentence "x is the new . . ." were typed
into Google (e.g., "Green is the new . . ." or "Bin Laden is the new . . .").

most dangerous man in America   Boardwalk Empire
        ↑   ↗ Snow White   ↓
LU   Julian Assange   → rebel with a cause   → Mad Men
  ↘ Banksy   ↓   Justified
  ↑   "catch me if   (Kim Cattrall from) Sex and the City
acie   you can"—figure
                                                     Sriracha
        offline → online   face for Olay   ↓
Jimmy Carter   Tau → Pi   Bacon
                                  Electro → Emo   ↓
–raw   Korean Movies → Tarantino   ↘ Techno   Lady Gaga
– retarded   pipelines → new boarders   ↑
   40 ← 30   less → more   Serato → Standard
   21 ← 18   on time ← early   Gigi Leung
wo Door Cinema Club → and Faster Phoenix or Vampire Weekend

Jesus ← Michael Jackson   Janet Jackson ← Janelle Monáe → Prince
   ↑   Justin Bieber   Bowie   Grace Jones
Farmville Know-Nothing Party
                                           mustache → beard
ty word ← Tea Party → Ku Klux Klan ← Islamic fundamentalism
 ↑   ↓   ↖
ancer   Jews   Book Burning   Whiskey → Wine ← Cheese
                                              ↑
  deranking   Craft Beer ← Coffee → Awesome!

       internet blocking   9-year-old Japanese kid   Mesut Özil
→ Foucault   ↓   ↙
Goa   Georgios Spanoudakis → Lionel Messi ← Javier Hernández

Here is a random selection.

WHY CITIES ARE THE NEW NATIONS

In 2002, the urbanist Richard Florida came forward with an interesting theory: Do people really follow jobs? Not any more, he claimed. Today, jobs follow people. Because of the close link between growth and creativity, there is a battle for creative talent. The winners of this battle will not be nations but cities and regions that can offer a combination of the "3 Ts":

- **Technology:** Growth needs technology. And high-technology centers offer attractive employment opportunities.
- **Talent:** Growth needs creative people—entrepreneurs, programmers, artists.
- **Tolerance:** Growth needs openness. Immigration and alternative approaches to life do not jeopardize future success (as Europe's neoconservatives like to claim) but are a condition for it. Change emerges from openness.

We want to add another "T" to these three factors:

Time Perspective: Florida also says: creativity is stimulated by exchange; it takes place in communities and real places. Therefore, it is not enough to throw a lot of creative people together, extract their creative energy and get new ones when they are used up. Creativity does not emerge in Skype conferences. Creativity emerges from relationships between people. If a company succeeds in retaining its employees for several years, trust, tolerance and creativity will develop. Incidentally, the same applies to people's relationships to cities and regions.

Where have you worked so far?
Where would you like to live?

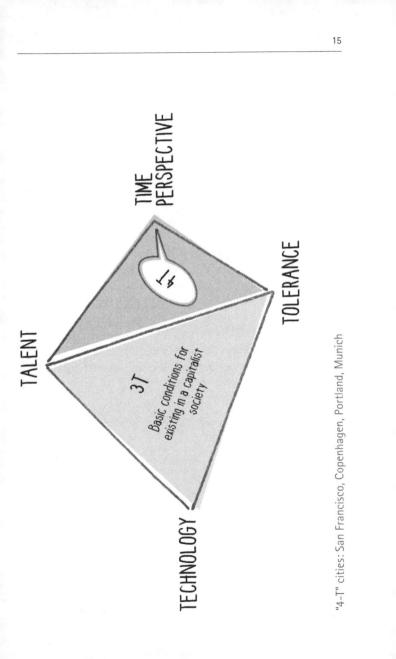

"4-T" cities: San Francisco, Copenhagen, Portland, Munich

HOW YOU CAN QUESTION EVERYTHING

Most models for explaining the world in human history are based on the idea that there is a nucleus, a defining moment, an origin, a beginning, a root from which everything developed in a linear fashion. First we lived in caves and discovered fire. Then we invented the wheel, democracy, the Enlightenment, human rights and the microchip. This development is often visualized in the form of a tree, with roots, a trunk and branches that grow toward the light—but no matter how numerous and intricate these branches become, they can all be traced back to a common starting point. This classical epistemological model, which is also called the "Tree of Life," is the foundation on which Western thinking has rested throughout its history: from Plato's *Diaeresis* and John Stuart Mill's *Homo oeconomicus* through to Freud's concept of the Oedipus complex, which claims that all psychological conditions can be traced back to one single traumatic moment (the separation of the child from the mother), to Chomsky's syntax tree.

One suspects that the tree metaphor is not very precise but it makes sense. It fits our way of thinking by identifying causes and effects. It fits our belief in progress: we always look up to people who are two steps above us rather than the other way around. Thus, development always occurs in a linear, bottom-up way, from a lower to a higher stage, from barbarism to civilization. The tree image fits our idea of roots: we need strong roots to be able to thrive. This idea is the foundation on which concepts like nationalism, origins, identity or the biological family as the basic unit of society rest.

The French philosophers Gilles Deleuze and Félix Guattari challenged the tree model. They argued that it is not open for change and that it presents a hierarchically structured system that determines what is a higher or lower stage of development. Instead, they suggested imagining life horizontally, not as a bottom-up process of development but as a decentralized movement in both directions. Their rhizome model shows an order in which all elements are interconnected and intersect but can nevertheless be independent of one another. The term "rhizome" comes from botany and refers to rootless plants like lilies of the valley, ginger or reseda. Some people say the internet has a rhizomatic structure. It is a huge network whose parts are connected to each other; it has no beginning and no end; there is no state of *being*, just a continuous state of *becoming*.

Four words to explain Deleuzian thinking are "horizontal rather than vertical." It is an irony of history that the cartographer of a horizontal structure of order ended his life voluntarily by performing a vertical fall out of his window.

Applying these ideas to ourselves, we could ask: is it conceivable that we do not stand on a ladder, i.e., that we don't develop vertically but horizontally? That we are not becoming better but just different?

"What is the point of roots if you can't take them with you?"
Gertrude Stein

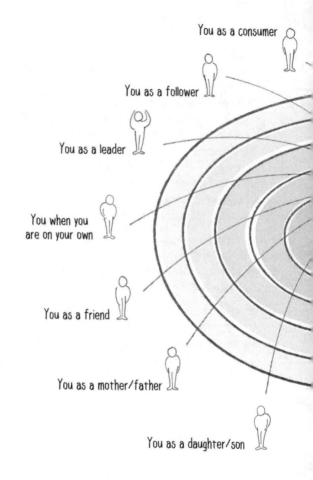

You as a consumer

You as a follower

You as a leader

You when you
are on your own

You as a friend

You as a mother/father

You as a daughter/son

Warning: This is not a rhizomatic depiction for it still has a center:
You. Look at the model and ask yourself: Who am I and how many?

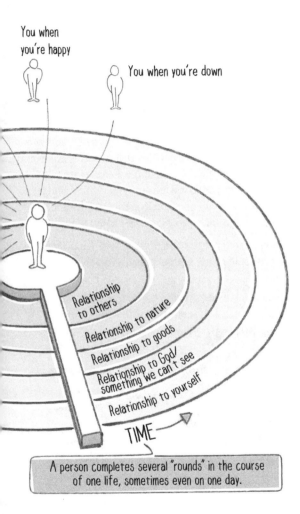

You when you're happy

You when you're down

Relationship to others

Relationship to nature

Relationship to goods

Relationship to God/ something we can't see

Relationship to yourself

TIME

A person completes several "rounds" in the course of one life, sometimes even on one day.

Can you imagine a world that you are not the center of? That has no center at all?

WHY AIR TRAVEL HAS BECOME SO CHEAP

In 1967 the lawyer Herb Kelleher sat with his client Rollin King in the St. Anthony Club in San Antonio. They were in the process of liquidating King's failed airline business. But King did not want to give up without a fight. He grabbed a bar napkin and a pen and wrote down the names of the three boom cities Dallas, San Antonio and Houston—and connected them in a triangle. Kelleher frowned: he did not yet know that he had just witnessed the birth of budget air travel. The greatest revolution of recent aviation was devised *on the back of a napkin*. What is the strategy of low-cost carriers?

- a limited number of direct connections between important cities, which should be as short as possible (point-to-point connections)
- avoiding hubs—too expensive, too time-consuming—and going to secondary airports (e.g., Luton instead of Heathrow)
- only one type of aircraft, short ground times (sometimes less than 30 minutes)
- only one service class, narrow seat spacing, no service, no lounges (no-frills concept)
- higher turnover through reservation of rental cars, hotel bookings, onboard sale of snacks (cross-selling)
- low ancillary wage costs, no trade union membership
- low ticket prices

We know this strategy from discount supermarkets: dispense with everything that was once believed to be indispensable.

Innovation means cutting out the unnecessary.

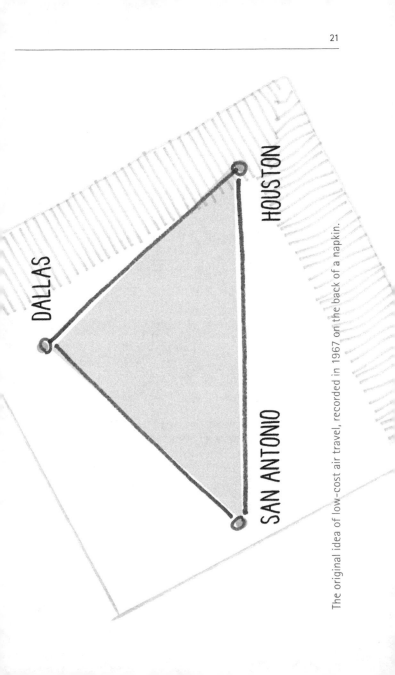

The original idea of low-cost air travel, recorded in 1967 on the back of a napkin.

WHAT THE WORLD WOULD LOOK LIKE AS A VILLAGE

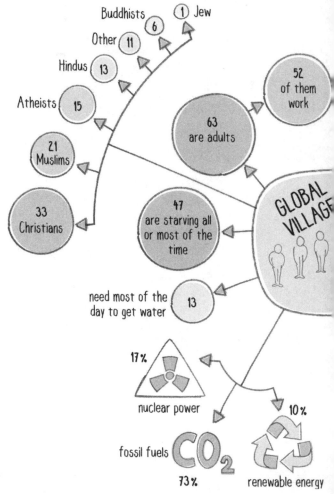

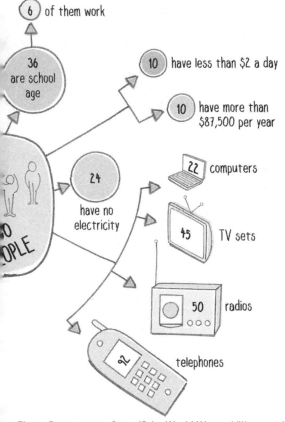

6 of them work

36 are school age

10 have less than $2 a day

10 have more than $87,500 per year

22 computers

45 TV sets

50 radios

telephones

24 have no electricity

...PEOPLE

These figures come from *If the World Were a Village* . . . by David J. Smith and Shelagh Armstrong

WHY WE SHOULDN'T TRUST OUR INSTINCTS

Four thousand car drivers want to get from A to D. There are two possible routes: 1) from A via B to D and 2) from A via C to D. AC and BD are motorways that bypass a mountain; the others are country roads. The journey time on each stretch of motorway is 45 minutes, regardless of the traffic. The journey time on the side roads, however, depends on the amount of traffic: it takes 10 minutes per 1,000 car drivers. The 4,000 drivers are divided up between the two routes. Two thousand drive ABD, the others ACD. The journey time for both routes thereby takes 65 minutes. The drivers complain about the slow-moving traffic. The intuitive solution: build a short tunnel through the mountains between B and C. But something surprising happens: the tunnel increases the average journey time.

The game theory approach of mathematician Dietrich Braess illustrates how this apparently sensible solution has the opposite of the desired effect. While apparently going against common sense, there is a fairly simple mathematical explanation:

If all 4,000 drivers take the apparent shortcut, the journey time is 80 minutes (4 x 10 plus 4 x 10 minutes—the drive through the tunnel is so quick it is insignificant). The journey around the mountain takes 85 minutes for each individual (45 minutes plus 4 x 10 minutes). The solution: don't use the tunnel and reach the destination in 65 minutes.

The Braess paradox reminds us that we should always question what we take for granted.

"Doubt is the beginning not the end of wisdom." *Proverb*

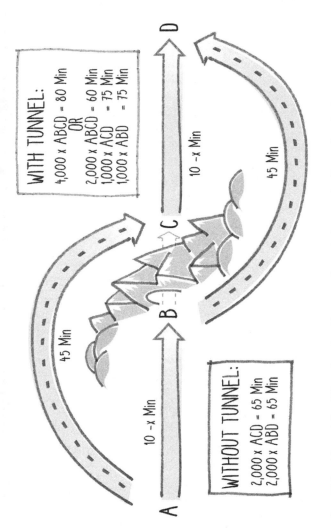

WITH TUNNEL:
4,000 x ABCD = 80 Min
OR
2,000 x ABCD = 60 Min
1,000 x ACD = 75 Min
1,000 x ABD = 75 Min

WITHOUT TUNNEL:
2,000 x ACD = 65 Min
2,000 x ABD = 65 Min

A

10 – x Min

B ----- C

10 – x Min

D

45 Min

45 Min

10 – x Min

Even if the drivers take different routes, the route through the tunnel will usually take longer.

WHY THE FREE MARKET DOESN'T WORK

George Soros is a speculator. He won his most lucrative battle in 1992, when he forced the British pound to its knees and consequently cashed in around a billion dollars. But Soros is also a social philosopher. From this double perspective he was able to explain why the "self-regulating" forces of the free market don't work. According to his boom-bust theory, the financial markets don't even think about moving toward the point of equilibrium to which they are logically and inevitably headed. Shares that jump in value result in overly optimistic investors and attract additional buyers (boom), which consequently cause prices to rise. If the market price moves too far from the realistic value, there is a price correction leading to a slump (bust).

In economic theory, deviations from the equilibrium are usually thought of in terms of a pendulum-like balancing process. Both types of movement—the pendulum gathering momentum, and the slowing down of the pendulum—can also be observed in reality: the slowing down of the pendulum tends to be connected with the production of commodities; its gathering momentum with the financial markets. Soros hits the nail on the head: financial markets tend toward excess. They work more like a wrecking ball than a pendulum.

"If you want to know what God thinks of money, just look at the people he gave it to." *Dorothy Parker*

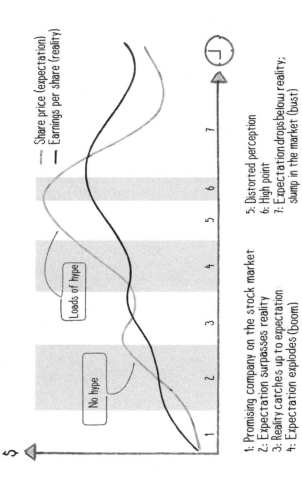

— Share price (expectation)
— Earnings per share (reality)

No hype

Loads of hype

1: Promising company on the stock market
2: Expectation surpasses reality
3: Reality catches up to expectation
4: Expectation explodes (boom)

5: Distorted perception
6: High point
7: Expectation drops below reality;
   slump in the market (bust)

When does the actual value of the company tally with its trading value?

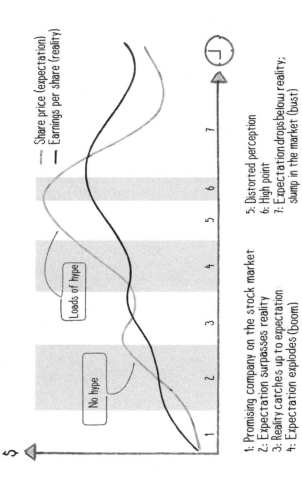

$

HOW IT HAPPENED

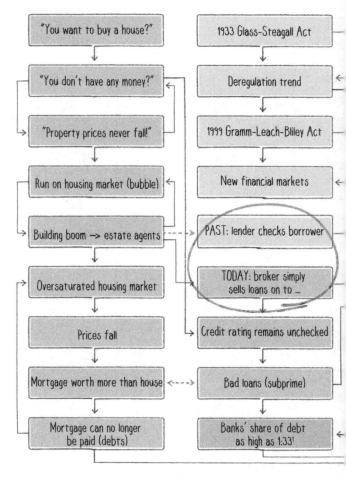

"You want to buy a house?"

"You don't have any money?"

"Property prices never fall!"

Run on housing market (bubble)

Building boom → estate agents

Oversaturated housing market

Prices fall

Mortgage worth more than house

Mortgage can no longer be paid (debts)

1933 Glass-Steagall Act

Deregulation trend

1999 Gramm-Leach-Bliley Act

New financial markets

PAST: lender checks borrower

TODAY: broker simply sells loans on to ...

Credit rating remains unchecked

Bad loans (subprime)

Banks' share of debt as high as 1:33[1]

[1] **Leverage ratio:** debt to equity ratio

[2] **Collateralized Debt Obligations:** derivatives, whose value depends on the future exchange rate of other shares

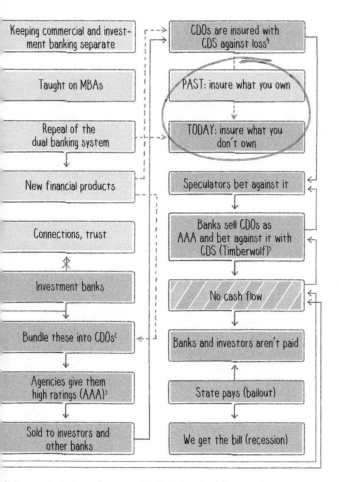

Keeping commercial and invest-ment banking separate	CDOs are insured with CDS against loss[4]
Taught on MBAs	PAST: insure what you own
Repeal of the dual banking system	TODAY: insure what you don't own
New financial products	Speculators bet against it
Connections, trust	Banks sell CDOs as AAA and bet against it with CDS (Timberwolf)[5]
Investment banks	No cash flow
Bundle these into CDOs[2]	Banks and investors aren't paid
Agencies give them high ratings (AAA)[3]	State pays (bailout)
Sold to investors and other banks	We get the bill (recession)

Rating agencies: banks pay agencies to rate CDOs

[4] **Credit Default Swap:** derivative that transfers credit risk from one party to another

[5] **Timberwolf:** derivative whereby the more money a customer loses, the more the bank earns!

WHO PAYS AND WHO EARNS

What it's about:
Corruption is the abuse of entrusted power for personal advantage. It can range from small facilitation payments to corruption networks. Corruption is not only ethically reprehensible, it also distorts competition: the resulting damages amount to an estimated billion dollars a year worldwide.

What you need to know:
Corruption involves at least two parties: the one who pays the bribe and the one who takes it. When it comes to large sums, there is usually a third party involved who hides the money, usually in an offshore financial center.

Our model shows these three forms of corruption based on data from the following globally recognized indices:

- Pay monies (BPI—Bribe Payers Index)
- Take monies (CPI—Corruption Perception Index)
- Hide monies (FSI—Financial Secrecy Index)

What you can do:
The most important weapon against corruption is transparency: transparent party financing, transparent administration and transparent reporting by multinationals. For example, it would be a start if mining and exploration companies were required to disclose payments made to governments of resource-rich countries.

"Corruption profits a minority in the short term, but everyone suffers in the long term. Let's exclude and ostracise those who don't want to understand this." *Dr. Christian Humborg, Transparency International*

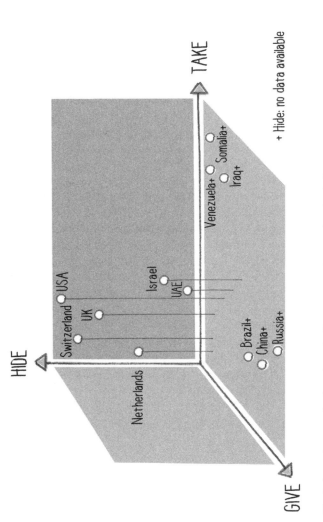

HIDE

TAKE

GIVE

Switzerland USA

Israel

UK

UAE

Netherlands

Venezuela+

Somalia+

Iraq+

Brazil+

China+

Russia+

+ Hide: no data available

The index values can be found on the Transparency International website.

WHO GOVERNS US?

Who should govern? The best person for the job, said Plato. His ideal state, as envisaged in the fourth century BC, was a republic ruled by philosophers like himself, with a warrior class to protect the state, and a producer class to serve it with services and skills. In Plato's republic, each citizen would have an occupation suited to his nature and abilities. And so that everything could take its just course, newborn babies would be taken away from their parents and raised by the state.

It took 2,300 years until Karl Popper radically contradicted this theory. In *The Open Society and Its Enemies* (1945), he depicts Plato as the father of the totalitarian state. Popper was the first voice to criticize not so much Plato's answer to the question "Who should govern?" but the question itself. According to Popper, it wasn't about developing a system in which the "best" ruled; the ideal system was one in which it was possible to get rid of bad rulers. Of course, it's possible to overdo the disposing: like the Italians, who have had sixty different governments since 1946, or the Germans prior to 1933, for whom the frequent changes of government, among other things, instilled a deep mistrust of parliamentary democracy. And yet the only form of government that enables a (relatively) painless removal of a bad government is democracy.

"In a democracy you say what you like and do what you're told."
Gerald Barry

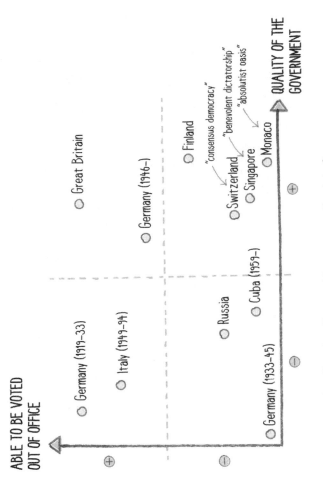

ABLE TO BE VOTED OUT OF OFFICE

Germany (1919–33)

Italy (1949–94)

Great Britain

Germany (1946–)

Russia

Finland

Cuba (1959–)

"consensus democracy"
Switzerland

"benevolent dictatorship"
Singapore

"absolutist oasis"
Monaco

Germany (1933–45)

QUALITY OF THE GOVERNMENT

This is a subjective allocation. How would you arrange the states?

HOW TO EXPLAIN THE WORLD TO ALIENS

On March 2, 1972, *Pioneer 10* was launched into space, the first space probe to leave our solar system. Although ostensibly highly scientific, the plan was at heart childlike: it was hoped that the probe would encounter aliens. For this reason, the astronomer Carl Sagan was commissioned with the creation of a 15 x 23-centimeter plaque explaining our world.

But how should we explain our world to aliens?

Sagan optimistically presumed that our physical laws also applied to aliens. So he drew the most common element in the universe, the hydrogen atom, based on the assumption that there was a universal unit of length (hydrogen emits radio waves with a wavelength of 21 cm). The web-like net in the center is the "pulsar map," a kind of cosmic map that shows the position of our solar system. The human couple is striking: the man is depicted with genitals, the woman without, both are Caucasian; the man has his hand raised in greeting to indicate humans' friendly intentions. Originally, Sagan wanted to depict the couple holding hands, but feared that aliens might then interpret them as a single being. Behind the couple is the outline of *Pioneer 10*, so that the finders of this message could estimate the size of humans in relation to the probe. At the bottom edge of the plaque is a diagram of our solar system: on the left, the sun; next to it the planets, and then another sketch of the launch of the probe from Earth.

In the 1980s, NASA experts discovered that an unknown force had diverted the probe in the direction of the sun. In 1997, *Pioneer 10* left our solar system at a speed of 12 km/s. Since February 2003 there has been no further trace of the probe.

How would you explain our world to an alien?

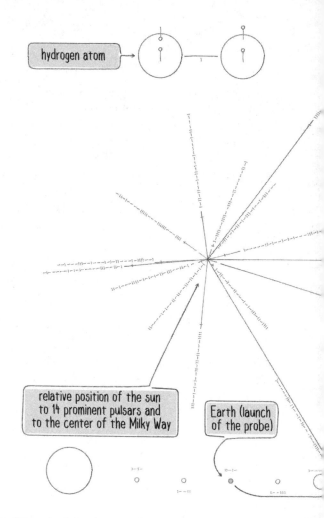

Many of the scientists who were shown this illustration were unable to decipher it.

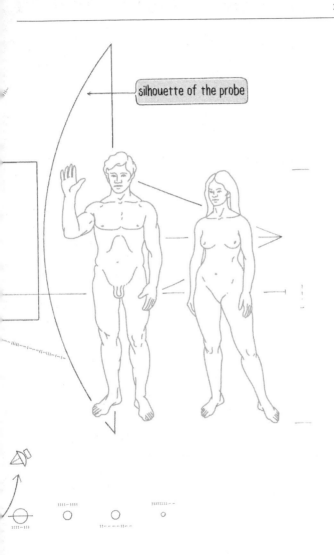

silhouette of the probe

WHY N = 3 AND M = 1

Here's a good question to casually drop into conversation with a scientist at a dinner party: Are there other "invisible" dimensions besides the three known spatial dimensions (length, width, height)? What you need to know in order to hold up your end of the conversation is that up until now there has not been a theory capable of explaining why we are able to recognize precisely three spatial dimensions. The relativity theory and the quantum field theory can be formulated for as many spatial dimensions as desired. If you're up to speed on the space-time debate, here is a good follow-up question: Why do we only have one dimension of time? The Swedish MIT cosmologist Max Tegmark researched the case with a time dimension, m=1, and a varying number of spatial dimensions, n. The result:

n < 3: insufficient complexity (no gravitation)

n > 3: insufficient stability (unstable solar system)

m < 1 or m > 1: insufficient causality (physics would lose its ability to predict)

What does this mean?
Recent theories suggest a "multiuniverse," in which the spatial and time dimensions vary from universe to universe. In his model, Tegmark concludes that our universe has three spatial dimensions and one time dimension—universes with other dimension ratios are probably uninhabitable.

Which is easier for you to imagine:
Having no space or no time?

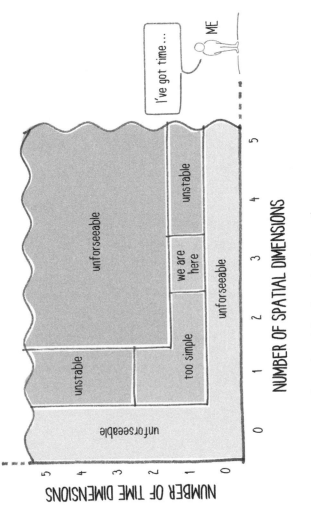

MIT cosmologist Max Tegmark explains dimensional space-time.

HOW WE KNOW WHAT WE THINK WE KNOW

Science stands for the eternal human quest for knowledge, power and recognition. Scientific methodology is the means to achieving these ends. There are two classic methodological approaches: the deductive and the inductive. With deduction you extrapolate the particular from the general. With induction you extrapolate the general from the particular.

Deduction:
- All people are mortal. (Rule)
- I am a person. (Case study)
- I am mortal. (Result)

Induction (using the example of a turkey):
- Turkey is treated well by humans. (Situation)
- Turkey continues to be treated well by humans. (Situation)
- Turkey is always treated well by humans. (Rule, only valid till day of slaughter.)

The danger of the induction method is that we can be led to a false conclusion even if we start out with the correct assumptions. For example, if the turkey is fed every day by the farmer, we cannot predict that the farmer will slaughter it one day. It makes more sense to challenge and modify an assumption repeatedly until it is irrefutable. In everyday life, though, we do the opposite: we develop a set of rules based on personal experience and then apply these to other experiences.

"Science is a cemetery of dead ideas."
Miguel de Unamuno y Jugo

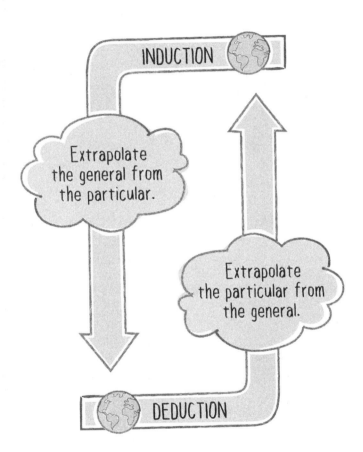

These are the two most prominent ways in which scientists work.

EXPLAINING MY WORLD

WHY SOME PEOPLE ARE UNFAITHFUL

Erick Janssen from the Kinsey Institute developed an infidelity matrix, the "Dual Control Model of Sexual Response" to explain human sexual behavior. He uses the analogy of a gas pedal and brakes to describe the dual forces of excitation (being easily attracted to another person) and inhibition (fighting this attraction). In order to find out how these two forces are balanced, Janssen designed a survey with questions such as: "If somebody you find sexually attractive accidentally brushes against you, are you immediately aroused?"

Janssen elicits whether, and how effectively, our brakes work, by asking, "If others can hear you having sex, do you quickly lose your desire?" or, "Do you lose your desire if you feel coerced into having sex?" This is where upbringing and convention come into play.

According to Janssen, around forty percent of people are easily aroused: their engines are revved. Which doesn't necessarily mean they are unfaithful, because only about half of these "racers" have trouble applying the brakes. You could call them two-timing cheats—or say that they live by a different value system such as polyamory, i.e., consensual nonmonogamy.

Twenty percent are "racers" who are also good at braking; they are faithful but feel the urge to go astray. The "solution": serial monogamy—promising undying love again and again.

"I never loved another person the way I loved myself." *Mae West*

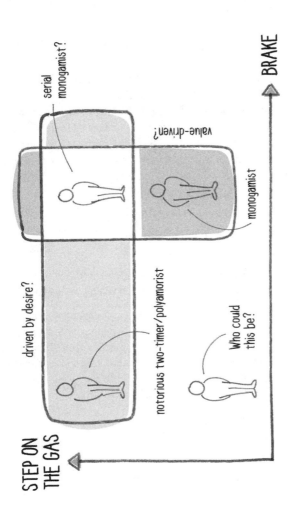

STEP ON THE GAS

BRAKE

driven by desire?

value-driven?

serial monogamist?

monogamist

notorious two-timer/polyamorist

Who could this be?

Where do you stand?

WHAT IT'S REALLY ALL ABOUT

What do we really want from life? Let's presume that most of us want happiness, money and to make an impact. If we don't enjoy what we do, we become unhappy. If we don't earn any money with what we do, we can't live. If what we do doesn't make an impact, it becomes pointless. How do we achieve all three? By aiming for the best possible result in our given situation. Economists call this budget restriction. How does it work? Add the dimension of time to the three goals. This creates four subgoals:

- **Short-term gain:** the income that you earn from doing a job
- **Long-term gain:** the knowledge and experience that you gain from a job
- **Short-term happiness:** the fun that you have doing a job
- **Long-term happiness:** the deeper meaning bestowed by a job

Whenever you have to make a decision—vocational training or university degree? children or career? children and career?—you can assess to what extent each option would contribute to the four subgoals. In the process you will also discover how important these four goals are to you and how close you have come to achieving them.

"When I was young, I thought money was the most important thing in life. Now that I'm old—I know it is." *Oscar Wilde*

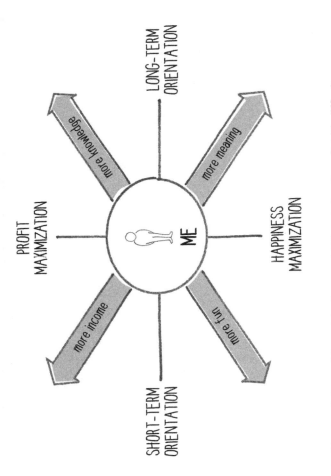

Of course it is possible to strive in several different directions. But it's difficult.

WHY PARENTS ARE UNIMPORTANT

"How the parents rear the child has no long-term effects on the child's personality, intelligence, or mental health."

When the psychologist Judith Rich Harris made this assertion in 1955, she became a persona non grata. But all she was really doing was questioning to what extent our personalities are shaped by our upbringing. Harris noticed that most studies which purported to prove the influence of parental nurture, neglected to analyze the importance of genetic influences. What's more, there were no studies on the interplay between parents and children—i.e., whether children elicit particular behavior in their parents and not just vice versa. According to Harris, the concept of "the family"—and its apparently profound influence on the individual—is a modern phenomenon. She contradicted the Freudians and development psychologists by suggesting that we modify our behavior depending on the environment we are in. Her conclusion: children are shaped not by their parents but by the peer group in which they are socialized.

Critics argued that her theory was an excuse for bad parenting. She countered: "Are you only loving towards your children because you think you can influence them?"

One of Harris' arguments: children speak the dialect of their peer group, not that of their parents. Critics retorted that parents determine their children's social environment by selecting their school for them, and therefore still have an influence.

He's a chip off the old block.

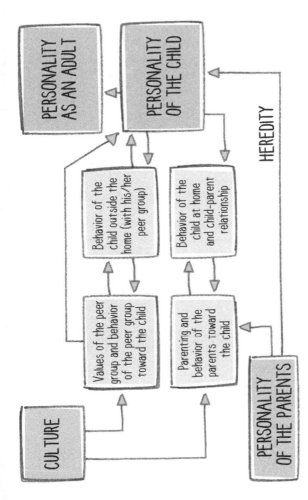

The group socialization model shows the effect of parenting and the influence of the peer group.

PERSONALITY AS AN ADULT

PERSONALITY OF THE CHILD

HEREDITY

Behavior of the child outside the home (with his/her peer group)

Behavior of the child at home and child–parent relationship

Values of the peer group and behavior of the peer group toward the child

Parenting and behavior of the parents toward the child

CULTURE

PERSONALITY OF THE PARENTS

WHAT WE THINK ABOUT OTHERS

Religion has always exploited prejudices. But what kind of prejudices do we have against particular religions?

A good tool for working this out is the Google algorithm. On Google.com you begin by typing in "Why are Jews . . ." With the help of the Google algorithm, the sentence is finished based on the search criteria of other users (for example: "Why are Jews so greedy?"; "Why are Jews so clever?") The algorithm is determined by the popularity of the search terms. In other words, all of the completed sentences resulting from your partial search were previously typed in as search terms by Google users.

This automatic completion (Google Autocomplete Results) is a revealing little method for gauging the interests and attitudes of Google users.

The model shown here reveals our results when we typed into Google "Why are . . ." adding one of the five world religions (Buddhists, Muslims, Hindus, Christians, Jews) and then we tried "atheists" and "Jehovah's Witnesses."

"If God exists, I hope he has a good excuse." *Woody Allen*

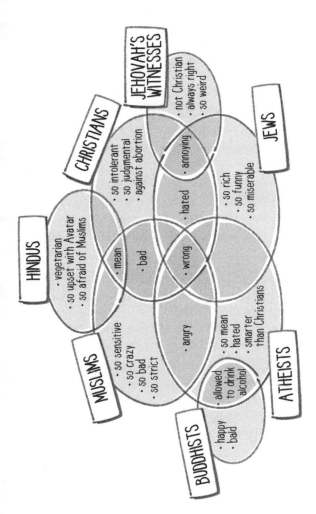

The algorithm always finds new prejudices. These are a selection from March 25, 2012, at approximately 10 p.m. Which ones do you share?

WHAT WE BELIEVE IN

Four observations at the start of the twenty-first century:

1. In English there will soon be more brands than words.
2. We are using more and more complicated channels and more and more money to reach fewer and fewer people.
3. Consumers are increasingly better informed about the things they buy.
4. There are some initial signs of brand saturation. And some initial reactions: In São Paulo every form of outdoor advertising has been banned. And, since 2009, the fashion brand Freshjive no longer uses its brand logo on its products.

What's going on here?

Hundreds of models have tried to explain how to win the battle for consumer attention in a saturated market. What none of these models wants to admit was noted by the communications expert Klaus Bernsau back in 2005: "Although everyone is talking about brands, there is still no universal and accepted brand theory."

Our trust in brands seems to be as unshakable and irrational as religious belief. Quietroom, the British brand language consultants, recently developed an unscientific model that shows how people's trust in the three brands "Santa Claus," "God" and "Socialism" change as they get older.

"The brand used to represent the company, now the company represents the brand." *Christoph Eschmann*

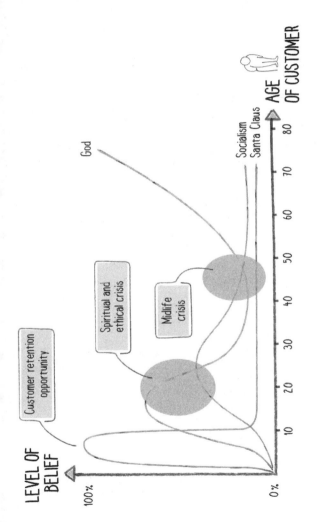

Add your own belief curves: marriage, capitalism, your success, your bank.

WHY YOU CAN'T BE AGAINST SOMETHING

Distinction theory claims that we try to stand out from the crowd by behaving differently to others. At the end of the nineteenth century, Thorstein Veblen coined the term "conspicuous consumption" to describe how consumers try to show off or raise their social status through consumption. Based on Veblen's *The Theory of the Leisure Class*, the Canadian Andrew Potter identified four phases of conspicuous consumption in the twentieth century and used these to describe the effect of counterculture in capitalism.

1. **"Keeping up with the Joneses"**
    The first half of the twentieth century saw the change from aristocratic to bourgeois consumption. The middle classes began to vie for status by trying to afford the same as their neighbors (the Joneses).

2. **"Anti-consumption"**
    Anti-consumption developed in the 1960s as a critique of the mainstream. The Swinging Sixties generation, the hippies, and later the punks, tried to deviate from the norm. They distinguished themselves from the mainstream through politics. The coolest were the pioneers of new (political) trends.

3. **Cool is mainstream**
    MTV and later the internet dissolved the (educational) elitism of counterculture. Suddenly it was possible for everybody to be cool and different. Because everybody had access to it, counterculture became mainstream. People thought they were different, when in fact they were like everybody else. It was the "uncool" who were suddenly—and unexpectedly—counterculture. *Cool* was dead.

4. "Authentic consumption"

However, the end of cool was not the end of conspicuous consumption. It was the birth of cultural capitalism. "Authentic consumption" incorporates the anti-consumerist aspiration. By consuming, you are not only doing something for yourself, but also for the environment, for the poor. An example: a Starbucks campaign claimed "It's not just what you're buying. It's what you're buying into." You aren't just buying a coffee anymore, you are supporting fair trade and fair working conditions. You are buying yourself out of the feeling of being a consumer.

The model on the following double page shows how counterculture works based on the example of Starbucks. The consumption of Starbucks coffee was considered mainstream in 2000. A counter-movement boycotted Starbucks and began buying fair trade coffee. For a brief moment these "rebels" considered themselves to be cool outsiders bucking the system—until Starbucks also started to sell fair trade coffee.

It could be that capitalism, as Engels and Marx predicted, has produced its own gravediggers. But so far, what we have seen above all is how capitalism has succeeded in assimilating every counter-movement going.

"Infinite growth of material consumption in a finite world is an impossibility." *E. F. Schumacher*

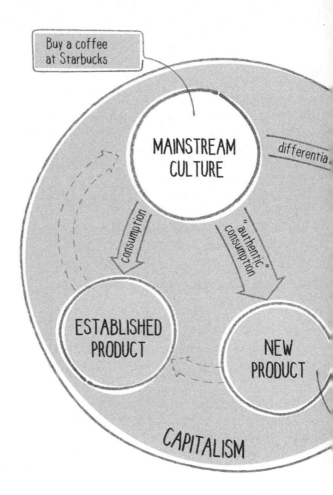

This model shows the attempt of counterculture to establish a
position outside of the system—and how capitalism integrates every
form of opposition and turns it into another market.

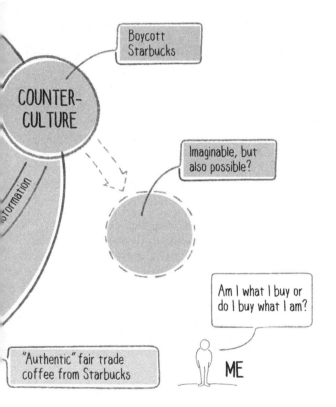

WHEN SOMETHING STARTS TO BE UNCOOL

Most of us spend a lot of time asking ourselves if we are doing the "right" thing: Are we wearing the right glasses? Do we hold the right views? Are we living in the right part of town? Have we given our child the right name? Everyone wants to be "cool." But what is "cool" exactly? It is actually hard to define. Cool is a kind of iconoclastic magic word. Once you define it, it isn't cool anymore. Cool is somebody who manages to be effortlessly unconventional, somebody who does or says the right thing without thinking about it. Because this *je ne sais quoi* often eludes us, we use status symbols to try to emulate it. And we are not just talking about teenage trends—every age group, every social class, every demographic group has its own status symbols, the mainstream to the same extent as the avant-garde.

In the U.S. there is a way of describing the point at which something becomes passé: it's *jumped the shark*. The saying was inspired by the TV series *Happy Days*, specifically an episode in which Fonzie tries to jump over a shark on waterskis. This ridiculous script idea suggested that the scriptwriters were literally losing the plot: they could no longer sustain the show's success and were resorting to cheap gimmicks in a desperate attempt to retain viewers. Initially applied to the beginning of the end of a TV series, the saying is now used more generally to describe the moment when something loses its freshness and starts to go downhill.

"What fun is it being cool if you can't wear a sombrero?"
Calvin and Hobbes

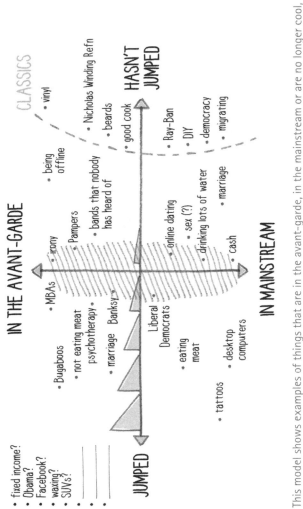

IN THE AVANT-GARDE

IN MAINSTREAM

HASN'T JUMPED

JUMPED

CLASSICS

- fixed income?
- Obama?
- Facebook?
- waxing?
- SUVs?
- ·······

- vinyl
- Nicholas Winding Refn
- beards
- good cook
- being offline
- Ray-Ban
- DIY
- democracy
- migrating
- bands that nobody has heard of
- online dating
- sex (?)
- drinking lots of water
- marriage
- cash
- irony
- Pampers
- MBAs
- Bugaboos
- not eating meat
- psychotherapy
- marriage Banksy
- Liberal Democrats
- eating meat
- desktop computers
- tattoos

This model shows examples of things that are in the avant-garde, in the mainstream or are no longer cool, i.e., that have "jumped." Right of the dotted line are timeless classics. What would you move around? What is irrelevant to you?

WHY WE DON'T LIKE FOREIGNERS

In 1992 Samuel Huntington predicted the clash of civilizations, the conflict between "us" and "them": the "other." The literary theorist Gayatri Spivak coined the term "othering" to describe the way in which we try to establish our own (positive) identity in relation to an inferior other.

The Western way of thinking is based on dichotomies: man/woman, human/animal, rationality/emotion and us/others. We need these others, or this otherness, to differentiate ourselves and to affirm our sense of self. Without otherness, there would be no opinion, no dialogue, and—in psychoanalytical terms—no self: we have to define an "other" in order to develop the self—or, for example, in childhood, to overcome the Oedipus complex (the child's desire for the mother). This basic pattern of differentiation between "us" and "others" takes a variety of forms: ethnic (black/white), regional (North/South), national (English/French), ideological (liberal/conservative), religious (Christian/Muslim), sexual (man/woman). The dichotomies in themselves are not the problem—of course there are differences. The problem is that opinions about difference are usually inherently judgmental: for example, the superiority of reason over emotion or civilization over wilderness.

"We have all a better guide in ourselves, if we would attend to it, than any other person can be." *Jane Austen*

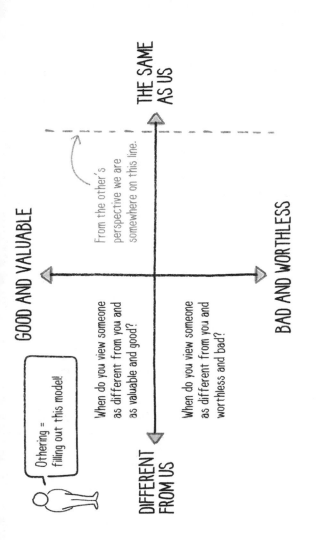

Othering is the separation of one group from another.

WHY A DVD BOX-SET IS THE MODERN EQUIVALENT OF A NOVEL

Watching a TV series is our way of escaping from reality. We want to know how the characters will develop, we want to share their neuroses and see into the depths of their souls, we want to be close to them in a way that we never are to ourselves. This model shows

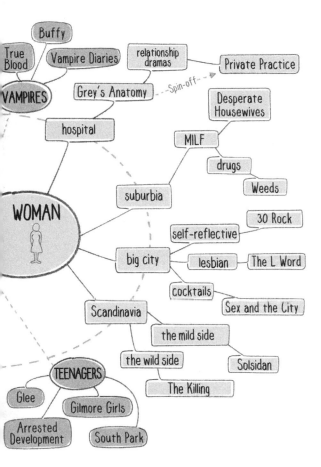

the subject and location as well as the sex of the main protagonists
of some of the most successful series of the last twenty years.
Which series are you currently watching?

Work is the curse of
the drinking classes.

Fashion is a form of uglines
so intolerable that we have
to alter it every six months

Experience is the name
we give to our mistakes.

Bigamy is having
one wife too many.
Monogamy is the same.

All women become
like their mothers.
That is their tragedy.
No man does. That's hi

AT THE BAR

Questions are never indiscreet,
answers sometimes are.

Everything
popular
is wrong.

Men marry because they are tired;
women because they are curious.
Both are disappointed.

The old believe everything,
the middle-aged suspect everythi
the young know everything.

EASY TO REMEMBER

The truth is rarely pure and never simple.

I am not young enough to know everything.

Always forgive your enemies, nothing annoys them so much.

When the gods wish to punish us they answer our prayers.

I think that God, in creating Man, somewhat overestimated his abilities.

The difference between literature and journalism is that journalism is unreadable and literature is not read.

America is the only country that went from barbarism to decadence without civilization in between.

Morality, like art, means to draw a line someplace.

There are only two tragedies in life: one is not getting what one wants, and the other is getting it.

AT THE QUEEN'S DINNER

LET ME THINK ABOUT IT

CHANGING MY WORLD

HOW YOU CAN MAKE THE RIGHT DECISION

Scenario: You want to buy a car. Problem: You can't decide which one to buy. Seven strategies—straight out of the labs of neurobiologists and psychologists:

1. **Decide on a research strategy.**
   Set yourself boundaries: e.g., one hour of internet research, ask three friends, read one car magazine, visit two car dealers.

2. **Limit your options.**
   The paradox of choice goes like this: we think that the bigger the choice, the better our decision. In fact, with a big choice, we spend too much time weighing up the options, so that at the end we may not reach a decision at all. The smaller the choice, the less we expect from the result.

3. **Accept "good enough."**
   Decide on something that meets your basic requirements instead of searching for "the best."

4. **Don't fear the consequences.**
   "The consequences of most decisions are not as lasting as we think," wrote the U.S. psychologist Daniel Gilbert. In the scheme of things, every decision loses importance.

5. **Go with your gut instinct.**
   In recent years there has been a lot of research into intuition. Two findings: it seems there is a part of us that knows more than we think we know. And, we tend to be more accepting of wrong decisions that we made impulsively, i.e., intuitively, than ones that we spent a long time thinking about. We forgive our heart more than our head.

6. Have someone else choose.

We tend to think that we are happier if we take things into our own hands. The opposite is true: Simona Botti from Cornell University has shown in experiments that when we make our own decisions we suffer nagging doubt that we didn't make the best choice. However, if another person decides for us, or if we toss a coin, we are either grateful or—if the outcome is bad—can blame someone else.

7. Don't question your decision anymore.

Or take a completely different approach: in the sixteenth century, the principal founder of the Jesuit order, Ignatius Loyola, came up with the following simple method for making the right decision: first, spend three days as if you had made a decision. During these three days, make a note of all your thoughts, feelings and dreams. Then go through the same process with an alternative decision. Compare your notes at the end. And then decide.

"All our final decisions are made in a state of mind that is not going to last." *Marcel Proust*

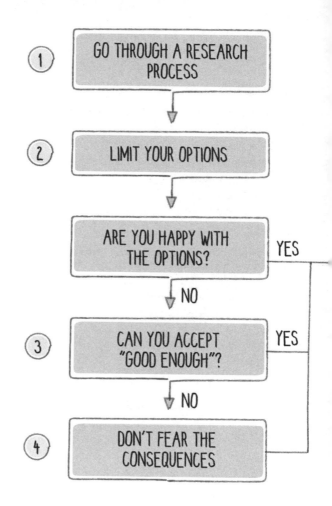

When did you last make the wrong decision?

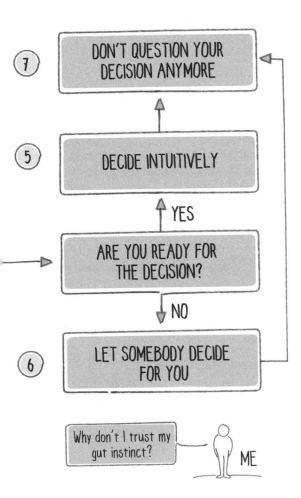

WHY WE LET OURSELVES BE DISTRACTED

Some disturbing facts and figures about our time: during a working day we visit an average of forty different websites. In the space of an hour we switch between the different programs on our computer thirty-six times. We consume three times as much information as we did thirty years ago. We communicate more via "the cloud"—email, social networks, online forums etc.—than directly with people. And if we don't reply to an email within a few hours or at the latest after a day, the sender gets angry—or forgets what they asked in the first place.

Every time we check our email or when we feel the familiar vibration of our phone in our pocket, we get a small dopamine injection in our brains. Over time this turns into an addiction, which results in us wanting this distraction more and more. So when we're bored or stuck, we check our mail or surf on Facebook. But every time we interrupt ourselves, we have to refocus ourselves afterward, which costs time and energy.

Of course, these technological achievements also increase our efficiency at work; Google Maps improves our punctuality; thanks to Skype and email we can work from anywhere; and Facebook is a brilliant marketing tool. But the point is: we have always equated computers with productivity. But when we look at our BlackBerry, we actually just give the impression of being productive. In fact we are distracting ourselves from work. We don't work more effectively with digital devices, we work faster. And more carelessly. We used to watch TV, today we watch our smartphone.

Four suggestions to avoid distraction overdose:

1. Read and answer emails for an hour at the beginning and end of your working day.

2. Have a no-email-Friday once a month.

3. Don't check your emails at all on Saturday.

4. Three times a year follow the "three-day rule." (After three days without the internet you begin to relax a bit. You might sleep more soundly. You might wait a bit longer before answering a question. Perhaps you'll listen more attentively.)

"We are always available, but also always distractable."
Matt Richtel

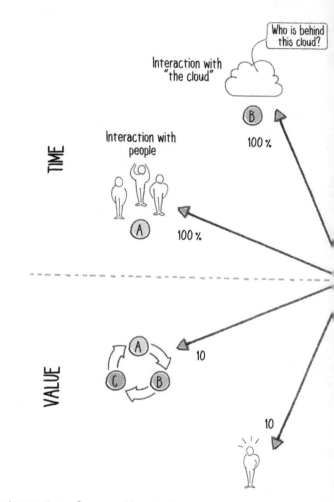

What percentage of your working day do you spend communicating offline with other people? What percentage in the cloud? For how much of the day are you fully concentrated on your work? How

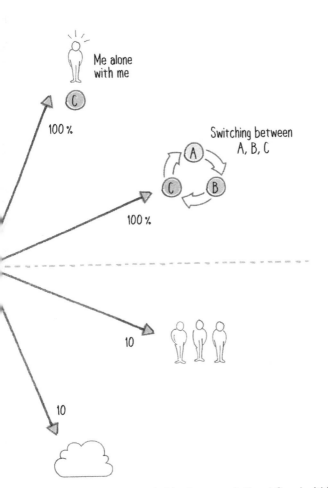

Me alone
with me

100 %

Switching between
A, B, C

100 %

10

10

much time do you spend switching between A, B and C and within C? Now, on a scale of 1 to 10, decide how important each of these activities is to you: 1 = unimportant, 10 = extremely important.

WHY WE DON'T HAVE ANY TIME

Every second, thousands of tweets are posted on Twitter and hundreds of thousands of status updates are posted on Facebook. At the same time people are receiving text messages, emails, and Skype or phone calls, and simultaneously consuming TV, radio and print media. It begs the question if we are able to react responsibly at all. After all, our brains can only process 40 bits/second—that's roughly equivalent to a seven-digit phone number.

No sooner have we submitted our dissertation proposal than a similar thesis appears on the net. No sooner does a momentous political event shake the world than global leaders are under pressure to react. The welcome effects of transparency and international cooperation are undermined by unsubstantiated rhetoric. There is no time for reflection: we live in a world of sound bites and half-baked information. It is pointless to pessimistically ask why everything is always getting faster. Time is moving at the same pace. The real question is: how do we divide up our time?

Most of us measure our life in years. Companies think in quarter years. Microsoft Outlook divides the day into 15-minute units. But how can we achieve and sustain our plans if they are dictated by such narrow time frames?

Christopher Patrick Peterka, founder of the communications agency gannaca, has suggested a clever way of escaping these parameters. He suggests giving up the conventional year model as a unit of time and dividing life into five-year rather than one-year units. So over a lifespan of 80 years this would mean 16 rather than 80 units.

Which means?

In the economy, everything depends on quarterly figures: long-term visions are subordinated to short-term goals and get lost in the fast pace of day-to-day business. There is even an expectation that major changes should be implemented right away. Nobody thinks beyond four months.

Planning over five years means planning beyond budget. A project can be executed in this time frame without it becoming the dominant focus. And plans that are not realized within this time should be fundamentally questioned. But above all: there are only 16 units of time at our disposal. The five-year-plan is not a model in the narrower sense, it is rather an invitation to throw away the diary and look at the horizon.

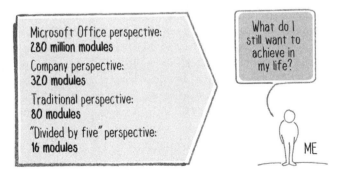

Microsoft Office perspective:
280 million modules

Company perspective:
320 modules

Traditional perspective:
80 modules

"Divided by five" perspective:
16 modules

What do I still want to achieve in my life?

ME

How many units do you still have at your disposal? And what do you want to do with them?

WHY WE AREN'T ALLOWED TO BE UNHAPPY

Question: Whose fault is it when you're ill, lonely, unemployed or unhappy? According to Marc Aurel, "happiness in life depends on the good thoughts that you have." This idea also underlies psychologist Martin Seligman's "happiness formula" H = S + C + V. Happiness is:

- ... genetic capacity for happiness, or "biological setpoint" (S)
- ... plus personal circumstances (C)
- ... plus factors under our voluntary control (V).

The U.S. author Barbara Ehrenreich, on the other hand, sees this formula as coercive and verging on militant: if you're unhappy it's your own fault because your attitude is not sufficiently positive. No matter what has befallen you—whether illness, unemployment or exclusion—you can turn things around if you really want to.

Does the way we think really make a difference? Most studies actually disprove that positive thinking can influence the healing process of diseases. Of course some people are helped by positive thoughts, but we are on shaky ground if we attribute all failures, illnesses or difficult situations to a lack of positive thinking. The sociologist Ulrich Bröckling also argues that we are increasingly subjected to a "self-optimization imperative," i.e., we feel permanently compelled to achieve more: to be more successful, more attractive, happier. This positive ideology implies that you're a failure if you don't work around the clock, achieve self-fulfilment, meditate, spend time with the children, cook for and have great sex with your partner, while remaining completely relaxed and happy.

What kind of an ideal is this? Bröckling calls it the "entrepreneurial self."

For Barbara Ehrenreich, this tyranny of positive thinking takes place not only in our private lives: the financial crisis as well as the war in Iraq are examples of the way in which positive thinking has got out of hand. Condoleezza Rice had serious doubts about invading Iraq but did not express them because George W. Bush hated to be "surrounded by pessimists." And in the run-up to the financial crisis, critics of derivatives were ignored or even laid off and rebuked for their lack of faith in the invisible hand of the free market.

What can we do?

Ehrenreich does not advocate boundless pessimism, but rather radical realism. It is not only "our decision" that counts. Our biological makeup, societal conditions, luck and fate—things that are completely out of our control—play a role too. So there are undoubtedly other reasons beyond ourselves why success eludes us or why we get ill.

What about you? On the following double page is a model of positive thinking. Follow the instructions and find out to what extent you have already internalized the idea of the entrepreneurial self.

"My life has no purpose, no direction, no aim, no meaning, and yet I'm happy. I can't figure it out. What am I doing right?"
Charles Schulz

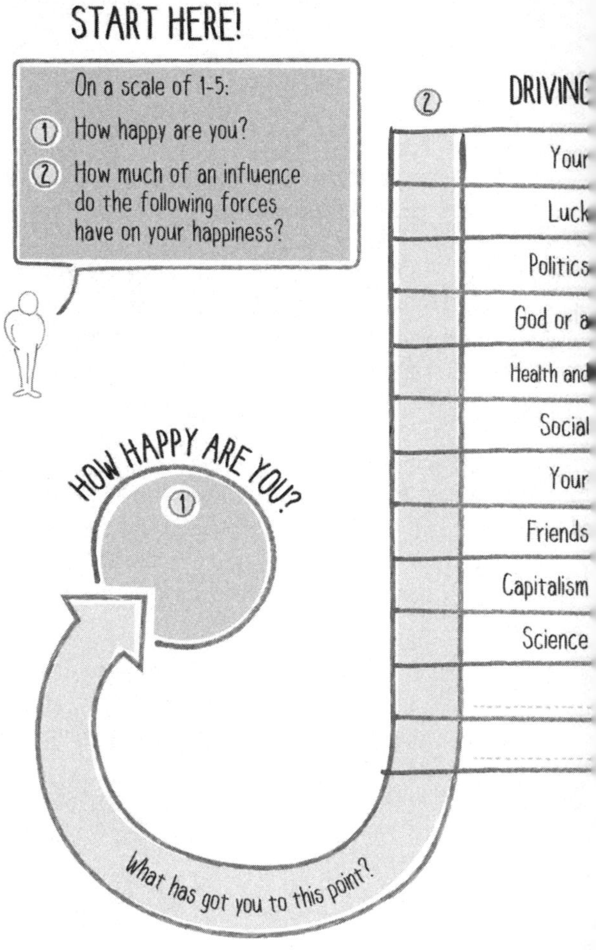

START HERE!

On a scale of 1-5:

1. How happy are you?

2. How much of an influence do the following forces have on your happiness?

HOW HAPPY ARE YOU?

1

What has got you to this point?

② DRIVING

Your

Luck

Politics

God or a

Health and

Social

Your

Friends

Capitalism

Science

After filling in: compare the values in column 2 and column 4. Are they the same? Why (not)?

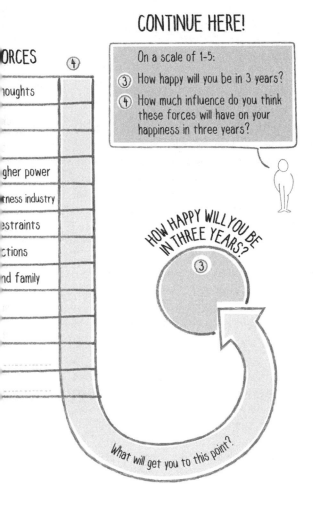

CONTINUE HERE!

ORCES ④

houghts

gher power

ness industry

straints

ctions

nd family

On a scale of 1-5:

③ How happy will you be in 3 years?

④ How much influence do you think these forces will have on your happiness in three years?

HOW HAPPY WILL YOU BE IN THREE YEARS?

③

What will get you to this point?

Option: Do the same but replace "happy" with "rich" or "lonely."

WHY CHANGE HURTS

Until the 1980s, change within companies was usually dictated from the top. The CEO made the decision, and the middle and bottom levels implemented it. The underlying values were control, consistency and predictability. The result: employees often did not know why something was being changed and also did not understand what was expected of them in the future. With the growing importance of psychology in business studies, a new approach to change emerged. Employees were no longer expected to submissively obey ("Of course!"), but to think for themselves ("Why are we doing that?"). The point was: change has to be understood if it is to be carried out effectively. Change management has developed into a discipline in its own right; today there are hundreds of models that deal with the subject, including pioneering ones like John Kotter's eight-stage model. But what most of them don't take account of is that change is rarely a painless process. Because change presupposes movement, which leads to friction. Friction causes pain. Every change—whether in a private or wider context—requires sacrifice and effort.

In reality, when the management of a company decides to make a change, it is usually other areas that bear the brunt of the pain. So we have to ask ourselves: if we want change, are we prepared to bear the pain that comes with it ourselves?

"Never too old, never too bad, never too late, never too sick to start from scratch once again." *Bikram Choudhury*

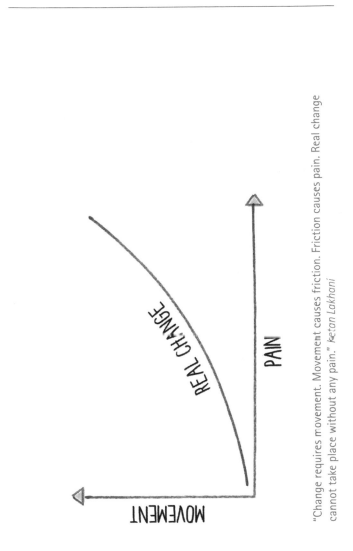

"Change requires movement. Movement causes friction. Friction causes pain. Real change cannot take place without any pain." *Ketan Lokhani*

WHAT WOULD TURN OUR SOCIETY UPSIDE DOWN

A thought about the social situation in western Europe: a third of the population lives comfortably, a third is afraid, a third has been written off. The welfare state—economists generally agree—is no longer affordable (or at least there are no convincing models as to how it could be financed). Wherever you turn, state-run institutions are being privatized in order to open up healthcare, social security and pension funds to competition. Since the politicians of the New Center in the 1990s (Clinton, Blair, Schröder) changed "welfare" to "workfare," there has been an increasing emphasis on taking personal responsibility for one's own well-being. We are witnessing how economic rationality is replacing notions of "social equality," "common good," or even "society." We are experiencing what the sociologist Nikolas Rose calls the "death of the social."

Inspired by this development is the idea of a basic income, a polemical as well as fascinating concept based on the idea that those who want to work should not be hindered and those who don't want to work should not be forced to do so. In concrete terms this means: every citizen receives a lifelong unconditional "income" from the state that is just enough to live off. Those who want more go and work.

Some possible advantages:

- There would be no more unemployment nor the social stigma attached to it.
- People would be free to do what they really wanted to do, which could result in added value.

- Work that nobody wants to do would have to become more financially attractive.
- The job market would be "freer"—employees and employers would be on equal terms.

Some possible disadvantages:

- Since only the citizens of a state would have a right to the basic income, there would be a restrictive immigration policy.
- As the most important financial provider, the state would transgress the liberal ideal of individual responsibility and create socialist-like conditions.

A few open questions:

- Would people become lazy if they were given money?
- Would the social divide become even wider?
- What would become of those who don't aspire to the entrepreneurial ideal?
- Above all: how could the basic income be financed?

"This reform is comparable to the abolition of slavery or the introduction of universal suffrage." *Philippe Van Parijs*

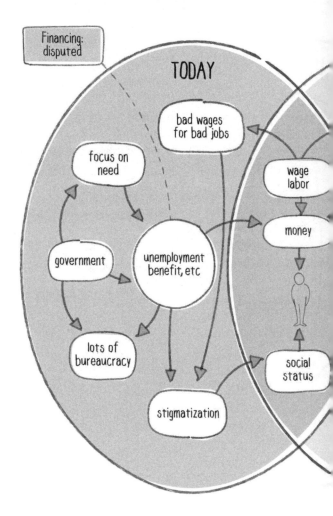

With the basic income, every citizen would be guaranteed an unconditional state income.

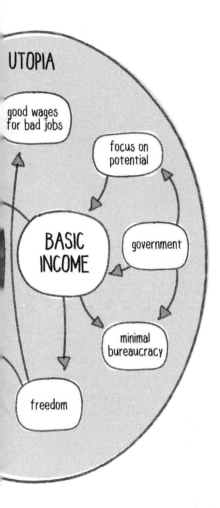

The model shows our current system (left) and the basic income system (right).

WHAT FUELS THE INTERNET

What are the biggest information-sharing internet applications, or Web 2.0 sites? And what drives them? A cautious assessment:

Google: as yet unrivaled algorithm

Wikipedia: voluntary participation—thousands offer their knowledge for free

WikiLeaks and others: desire for transparency

Facebook: desire for relationships and recognition

But the biggest—underlying—driving force is the fact that nearly everybody today willingly makes their private data public. It's called "default to public": everything that we don't explicitly declare as private is automatically public. Such a change is unprecedented in our history, which is why there are still many unanswered questions. What can be done with these structures? And what—apart from advertising purposes—are they used for? Why do we disclose our personal details for free when we could sell them for a lot of money?

The Web 2.0 works because we are willing participants. For digital natives, i.e., the generation that cannot remember a time before the internet, this is normality. They also can't remember the first time they met their online acquaintances offline. They don't distinguish between online and offline. The difference is irrelevant to them. It is void.

Today the most interesting people are those that we can't find on Google.

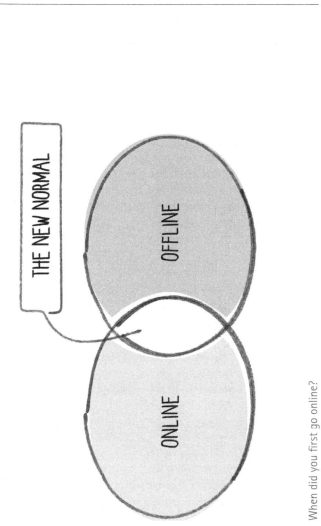

THE NEW NORMAL

OFFLINE

ONLINE

When did you first go online?

HOW JESUS WOULD INVEST

There's no way around it: capitalism is the all-dominating economic system of our time. It is *the* system. But it's stuck in a crisis. In a world in which Nobel prizes are awarded for financial derivatives (Black-Scholes formula); in which banks can lend nine euros for every euro they receive; in which neither customers nor sellers understand the products that they are dealing with—the question has to be asked: can we even trust the rules of the game?

A number of Western economists regard "Islamic banking" with a mixture of curiosity and envy: a tightly controlled banking sector based on religious laws (prohibition of interest, ban on specula-tion, ban on investment in alcohol, prostitution, pork, etc.) What is surprising is not that this system works—and made it through the financial crisis relatively unscathed—but that there is no equiva-lent in Western capitalism despite an interest in sustainable, ethical investment. This then begs the question of whether the West would even be capable of establishing an ethical banking sector. And if so, based on what principles? On Christian ones, says Paul S. Mills, an economist at Cambridge University. It's worth thinking about his model.

Mills establishes four basic rules that cannot be broken with a Christian investment:

1. **Be informed:** Do you know what happens with your invested money? The globalized financial market functions according to the principle: what you don't know won't hurt you. Problematic information is kept at a deliberate distance.

2. **Take responsibility:** What are you earning your money with? The Bible is not against profit, but it should not be earned

at the cost of others. Rule of thumb: it's better to earn with transactions (money in exchange for service/goods) than with interest. Purchasing a property to let is acceptable, but don't speculate with it. Don't reap what you did not sow (Luke 19:22).

3. **Take risks:** Money that's lying around—even in a bank account—has a limited use-by date. Money has to be invested, so that others can profit from it. That you could lose in the process is part of the gain. Through a loss you gain *sancta indifferentia*, holy indifference (Luke 10:35).

4. **Practice humility:** Hands off put options (security against a slump in the market)—we should not insure ourselves against the will of God.

"Not everything that is legal is also legitimate." *Josef Ackermann*

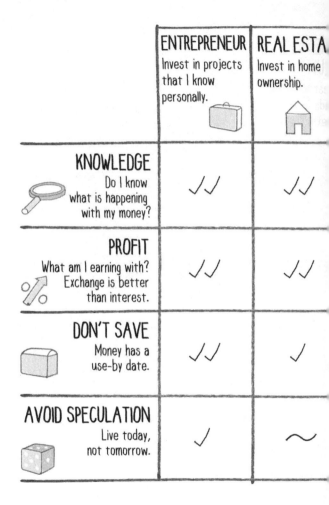

	ENTREPRENEUR Invest in projects that I know personally.	REAL ESTA Invest in home ownership.
KNOWLEDGE Do I know what is happening with my money?	✓✓	✓✓
PROFIT What am I earning with? Exchange is better than interest.	✓✓	✓✓
DON'T SAVE Money has a use-by date.	✓✓	✓
AVOID SPECULATION Live today, not tomorrow.	✓	~

Think about your own assets in relation to these basic rules and ask yourself: How do I invest? How do I feel about it? What would have to happen for me to change the way I invest?

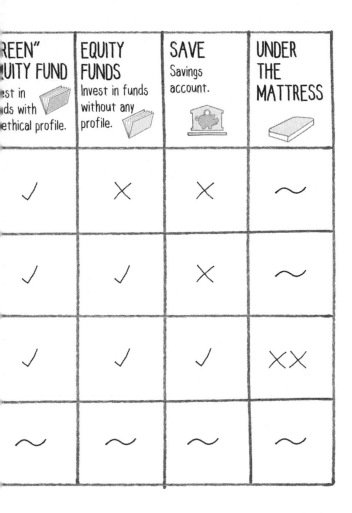

"GREEN" EQUITY FUND Invest in funds with ethical profile.	EQUITY FUNDS Invest in funds without any profile.	SAVE Savings account.	UNDER THE MATTRESS
✓	✗	✗	~
✓	✓	✗	~
✓	✓	✓	✗✗
~	~	~	~

Here's how to read the model: double check = sensible; one check = acceptable; x = dubious; wave = not applicable.

HOW WE DEAL WITH DYING

In her model "The Five Stages of Dying," the Swiss psychiatrist Elisabeth Kübler-Ross (1926–2004) described the process a person goes through after being told that they are dying:

1. **Denial**—"I'm fine."
   The dying person represses the diagnosis: she looks for another doctor in the hope of a "better" diagnosis.

2. **Anger**—"Why me?"
   The dying person directs her rage at everyone who is able to continue living—relatives, caregivers.

3. **Bargaining**—"I would give anything to live for another year."
   The dying person accepts her impending death, but begins to "negotiate"—with doctors, with God, with fate. She tries to buy time.

4. **Depression**—"I'm going to die, nothing matters anymore."
   The dying person becomes disconnected, refuses visitors. Psychologically speaking, this phase allows her to take leave from the people she loves.

5. **Acceptance**—"I can't fight it, I might as well prepare myself for it."
   The dying person comes to terms with her mortality.

"What's going to be your best memory of earth? What one moment for you defines what it's like to be alive on this planet?"
Douglas Coupland, "Generation X"

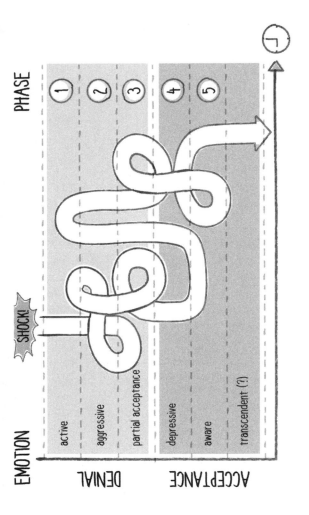

The five stages of dying can last for different periods of time, some may be skipped or be repeated.

WHY THERE IS NO TRUTH

Imagine there was no objective truth. Imagine that the things we accept as true, based on objective evidence—such as the theory of evolution, free will, the differences between humans and animals—are in fact just expressions of particular interests or power relations.

Some of the most radical forward thinkers thought exactly this and came to the conclusion that "scientific objectivity" is an ideological construction. Not that these critics suggested an alternative in the form of God or another truth. Rather, they questioned the validity of truth itself.

To clarify: those who strive for objective knowledge try to explain the world "as it really is." They apparently stand above economic or political interests, so their "unbiased" research findings are free of claims to power and detached from the social situation in which they were made. This seeing from "nowhere"—or infinite vision from all perspectives—is called the "God trick" by the forward-thinker Donna Haraway, i.e. it is impossible.

Because, argue critics of objectivity, to see the world "as it really is" is innately biased. An example: if we think of prehistoric man, we imagine powerful, spear-wielding men hunting giant mammoths. For a long time this image was regarded as objectively true in scientific circles—and in some children's books it still is. In fact, this clichéd image originated in the nineteenth century, a time when hunting was a prestigious pastime, which is why the archaeologists, in their interpretations of prehistoric life, ignored the less spectacular forms of food procurement. They weren't objective; they took a perspective that presented the role of the man as provider and warrior as a kind of natural law. Similarly biased perspectives were used to justify theories about race that up to a hundred years ago were still accepted as objectively true. And with regards to current neurological research, we could ask: why is research primarily done into the differences between male and female brains? Which gender roles are these studies trying to cement? It would be just as easy to research similarities between male and female brains.

Doubting objectivity does not mean asking what is right or wrong. The question of what is true or untrue is meaningless, or rather it is wrongly formulated. It makes more sense to ask: What is *considered* to be true? And who profits from it? Someone who claims to "speak the truth" should ask himself: what are the conditions in which this truth is being produced? In fact this also applies to the critique of objectivity itself.

And now? Begin by stopping. Stop believing every study you read. Stop believing every platitude ("Capitalism needs growth," "education is key"). Stop believing that there is such a thing as objectivity—you will always find somebody who thinks exactly the opposite is "objectively" true. Start to be curious—and critical—about the attitudes of others and about your own.

"Why truth? Why not lies?" *Friedrich Nietzsche*

CHANGING OUR WORLD

WHO RULES THE WORLD

Consider the world order since 1945: the Cold War was defined by the bipolar competition between the USSR and the USA. Out of this arose an intermediate G-1 phase with the USA as the only super-power. This was followed by the era of the multipolar leagues G-6 to G-20. The European and the African Unions developed during the same period. The idea behind these alliances is that countries that trade with one another and are united in leagues won't fight each other. "Pipelines are the new borders" is the motto of the new league proponents.

However, some political observers have identified two new, completely different order logics:

1. **New players**

    The twenty-first century will not be dominated by Brazil, China or the USA but by "the city," "the company" and "the organization." Years ago, the social scientist Susan Strange already predicted a triangular diplomacy between countries, leagues and companies. Cities and regions (Istanbul, California, Songdo City), companies (Royal Dutch Shell, Gazprom, Facebook—which is, after all, the third biggest "nation" in the world) and NGOs (Bill & Melinda Gates Foundation, Club of Rome, Greenpeace, as well as IOC and FIFA), are better linked, more cleverly positioned, and less bureaucratically structured than nations or leagues such as the EU, UN or WTO.

2. **No more alliances**

    The twenty-first century will be dominated by a G-0 system. The failure of Kyoto, Copenhagen and Cancún is a portent of this development: not even the need to conserve the means of our existence is a strong enough argument to reach a multilateral agreement. There are no more common overarching interests, only temporary alliances. Each for his own. We can see it happening already: Asia will use its economic position to political advantage, old Europe won't give up its hegemony without a fight. In a G-0 world, politics would govern trade. And as David Bosshart, head of the Swiss think tank GDI, writes, there would always be a danger that conflicts turn into wars: currency wars, agricultural wars, speculation wars, government bond wars—or hot wars.

And what is the role of ordinary citizens in this new order? U.S. economist Robert Reich: "For a long time we believed that democracy and capitalism were inseparable from one another. Today we know this is no longer the case." Individual freedom is the cornerstone of capitalism? Once upon a time. The emerging nations have replaced democracy with a new definition of social justice: they promise their citizens work, an income, freedom to travel, consumption—and deprive them of the possibility of political involvement.

We asked political scientists to assess global conflicts in terms of a knockout tournament. The results can be found on the following page. Who will win?

"Old, white, male, sated versus young, Asian, female, hungry."
David Bosshart

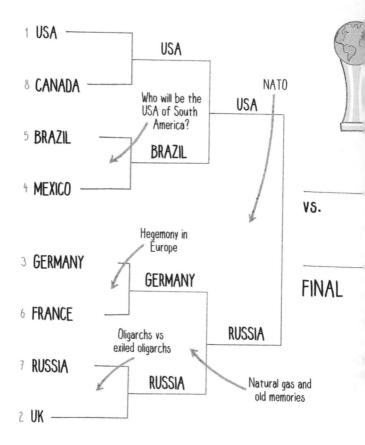

Beware: This is not the New World Order. This World Cup Chart shows playfully some potential new conflicts in a G-O World Order.

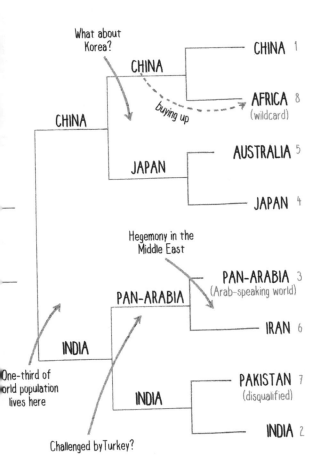

WHY YOU SHOULD TELL THE TRUTH

Just as communism, as conceived by Karl Marx and Friedrich Engels, threatened to topple the political and economic system in 1848, so it was Julian Assange's whistle-blowing, WikiLeaks, which threw international politics into turmoil in 2010. The USA was left floundering when WikiLeaks revealed details of U.S. action in Iraq—and Assange's announcement that he would leak email exchanges from a major bank was enough to make share prices plummet.

When Eric Schmidt was still head of Google, he said that anyone who didn't want something that they had done to become public had better not do it in the first place. He meant private individuals; WikiLeaks applied this rule to governments, state institutions and companies. Whistle-blowing shouldn't really be necessary. In business as well as in politics there are sophisticated transparency and control mechanisms: accounting standards, codes of commercial law and corporate government codices, as well as the classic division of power between legislative (parliament), executive (government) and judicial (courts of law). However, for a long time this model has not worked in the way that Montesquieu envisaged it—because governments are usually formed by the parties that also hold the majority of seats in parliament.

As a result, a fourth power emerged in the twentieth century: the media, a supervisory body that for a variety of reasons works imperfectly. A few reasons are:

- Personal proximity: journalists that report on the parties or companies are often on close personal terms with the people involved. You don't dig the dirt on someone you know.

- Economic dependence: companies use the media to advertise; politicians give journalists access to information. Or not. Media that want to stay in business have to make compromises.
- PR: politicians and companies have developed sophisticated strategies to control journalists. They know exactly to whom they can say what, when and how, so that the subsequent coverage in the media is along exactly the right lines.

In the twenty-first century we seem to be ready to add a fifth power to these four intertwined powers: the destructive. This isn't a pillar, it's a bomb that, regardless of the consequences, can destroy any of the other powers that abuses the authority with which they have been entrusted. WikiLeaks was only the beginning.

And now? If you head a company or a department, take a moment to think about the example of Alex Bogusky, once regarded as one of the top advertisers in the U.S., who from one day to the next pulled out in order to fight in the corner of the consumer:

"Becoming transparent isn't a choice. The only choice is: do you do it, or do you have it done to you? And please don't make the mistake of trying to be a little bit transparent. Take the aspect of your business you feel you would least like to get PR on and make a plan to tell your customers how you hope to address the issue. And ask them for help along the way. Your customers are ready and anxious to join your mission if you let them."

"Stopping leaks is the new form of censorship." *Julian Assange*

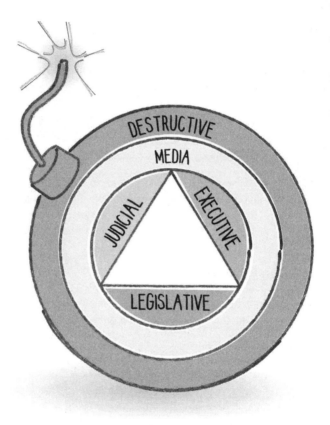

Division of power 2012: judicial, legislative, executive, media, destructive.

NOW IT'S YOUR TURN:

1. What do you lie to yourself about?

   _____

2. What do you lie about to your partner?

   _____

3. What secrets do you have?

   _____

   Which of these could absolutely not be made public?

   _____

4. Is there an issue that you have avoided confronting for a long time?

   _____

   What?

   _____

5. Have you ever abused your power?

   ☐ Yes ☐ No

6. Where do you wield power?

   _____

   Who gave you this power?

   _____

7. Do you know something that you are deliberately keeping to yourself although you sometimes think you should tell others about it?

   ☐ Yes ☐ No

   How do you justify this to yourself?

   _____

WHAT WE NEED TO DEFEND OURSELVES AGAINST

The second decade of the new millennium will go down in history as the decade of revolutions. They began in the Arab region and their energy was as infectious as their consequences were unclear. Only one thing is certain: a new generation is showing us that there is another way. That an existing order can be overthrown. That change is never brought about by systems but always by people. That ultimately we are the ones who can bring about change if we are only willing to fight for it.

And what about us? What are the dictatorships of a "free world"? Inspired by the small Facebook group TANK, which sprang up during the Egyptian revolution, this model identifies six dictatorships that have to be toppled.

1. **Dictatorship of fear:** a new world has to be a bold one.

2. **Dictatorship of growth:** neoliberalism is only an idea, not a law.

3. **Dictatorship of breaking news:** if a piece of news is so important, we will hear about it anyway. Instead, attention should be drawn to what is overlooked.

4. **Dictatorship of health and beauty:** don't let body image rule your life.

5. **Dictatorship of irony:** we need to take the things we do seriously.

6. **Dictatorship of love:** allowing freedom is the next stage of coupledom.

"When dictatorship is a fact, revolution is a duty." *Victor Hugo*

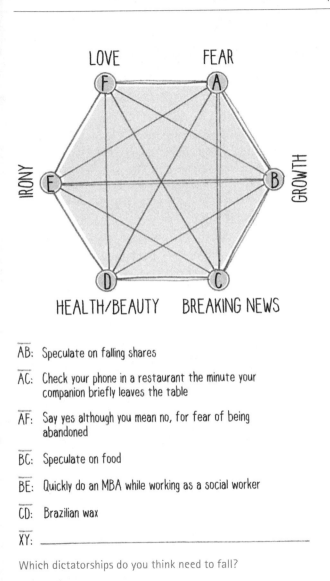

AB: Speculate on falling shares

AC: Check your phone in a restaurant the minute your companion briefly leaves the table

AF: Say yes although you mean no, for fear of being abandoned

BC: Speculate on food

BE: Quickly do an MBA while working as a social worker

CD: Brazilian wax

XY: _____

Which dictatorships do you think need to fall?

HOW TEAM MEMBERS PARALYZE EACH OTHER

How free are we in the decisions that we make? Not at all, according to most studies. During the 2008 financial crisis, customers of the financial institution Washington Mutual withdrew over 16 billion dollars from their accounts within a matter of days—simply because they had heard that this is what other people were doing. The phenomenon is called herd instinct.

Another form of collective behavior is swarm intelligence, familiar to us from ant algorithms. On first sight the ants in a colony appear to be moving around completely randomly, but if you look closer, a pattern can be seen. The "swarm" finds the shortest route to the best source of food, allocates tasks, defends territories. Based on this observation, Professor Marco Dorigo solved a variety of logistics problems: truck routing, slot allocation at airports, controlling of military robots.

But it is debatable whether this sort of ant algorithm also works with groups of people, because it does not take into account the "human" side of swarm intelligence: group thinking. In homogenous groups, opinions and viewpoints can intensify and become cohesive very quickly. And if too many people are too sure of the same thing, attitudes can become radical and actions rash. Researchers have observed this phenomenon with juries: the more united a jury is, the harsher the sentence and the more convinced the members of the jury are that their verdict was the right one. It is a kind of uncritical consensus: if everyone else does the same as you, you believe you are in the right.

"Why do we follow the majority? Is it because they have more reason? No, because they have more power." *Blaise Pascal*

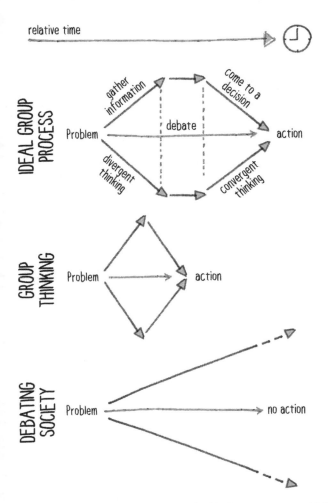

relative time

IDEAL GROUP PROCESS

gather information · come to a decision

Problem — debate → action

divergent thinking · convergent thinking

GROUP THINKING

Problem → action

DEBATING SOCIETY

Problem → no action

Three forms of finding a consensus: the ideal process, group thinking and the endless discussions of debating societies.

WHY WE (DON'T) STOP BELIEVING

The crucial question of the twenty-first century is: what do we believe in—and for how much longer? Religion, in the collective sense, is in sharp decline in the Western world. The Swiss Religious Studies professor Jürgen Mohn has noticed three interrelated currents that have become more intense since 9/11:

1. **Individualization of religion ("pick'n'mix")**

   Institutional religion is increasingly perceived as a public nuisance. Some studies predict that by 2020, only twenty percent of west Europeans will still be members of a church. Which doesn't mean that everyone else will be atheist. The rejection of the church goes hand in hand with a private spiritual reorientation: individual religions based on a kind of "pick'n'mix" approach (eclecticism). You help yourself from a variety of beliefs, mix heathen rituals with Christian traditions, mysticism with feel-good spiritualism. The victor in this development is Buddhism, the first religion to gain followers without a missionary crusade.

2. **"Religionization" of politics ("Axis of Evil")**

   The events of 9/11 signaled the end of the "secular era" of the global modern world. The democratic missionary zeal took on religious overtones. The language of politics began to reintroduce Old Testament terms ("axis of evil") and legitimization strategies (revenge). In Europe, Islam was countered by a "Christian-Jewish-enlightened" civil religion. The question is, now that religious thinking and rhetoric has been (re)discovered as a means of legitimizing political and military action, will it replace territorial thinking?

3. **Market orientation of religion ("Ayurveda," "Apple disciples")**

   Religion is no longer state-controlled, it is market-controlled.
   Free churches, sects and alternative religions are growing
   in popularity. Spirituality is a business sector, Ayurveda its
   metaphor. So it is only logical that brands also need to create
   and propagate a "corporate religion" to appeal to consumers.

"Thank God I'm an atheist." *Luis Buñuel*

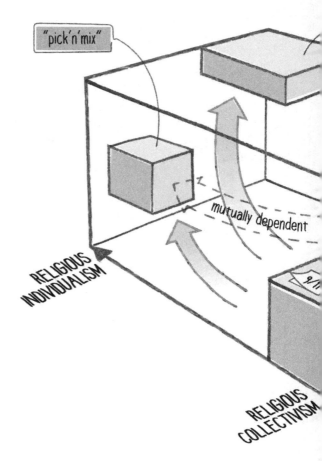

"pick'n'mix"

mutually dependent

RELIGIOUS INDIVIDUALISM

RELIGIOUS COLLECTIVISM

9/11

The search for new communities is destroying the old ones, but spiritual belief as such is not disappearing.

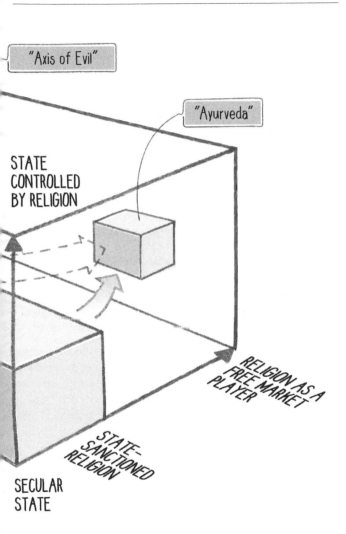

"Axis of Evil"

"Ayurveda"

STATE
CONTROLLED
BY RELIGION

RELIGION AS A
FREE MARKET
PLAYER

STATE-
SANCTIONED
RELIGION

SECULAR
STATE

HOW WE CAN INTERVENE IN OUR FUTURE

How do you make your way in a world that is changing at an unprecedented rate? In 2002, the U.S. government gave a surprising answer to this question. In light of the possible existence of weapons of mass destruction in Iraq, it was necessary to tackle the situation *preemptively*: "America will act against emerging threats before they are fully formed."

Acting preemptively not only contravenes international law, which forbids anticipatory attacks, it also marks a rupture with conventional forms of prevention. Prevention means preparing for a future that you expect and for which you want to be prepared. Preemption constitutes an action that acknowledges the unpredictability of the future. Rather than acting preventatively, you participate in the coevolution of an event. You do not prepare for change, you fuel it —based not on secure knowledge but on speculation, wishes, fears.

This principle has already found its way into other areas of society. One example is the weather. At the Olympic Games in Beijing in 2008, silver iodide was blasted into the sky to ensure dry weather for the opening ceremony. This geoengineering, i.e., geochemical intervention in nature, is symptomatic of how the strategy of preemption has moved beyond the field of war and infiltrated civil life.

"The trouble with our times is that the future is not what it used to be." *Paul Valéry*

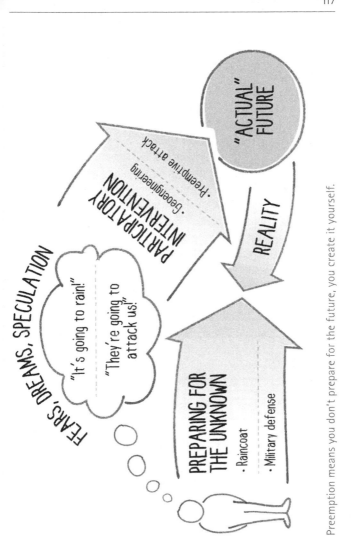

Preemption means you don't prepare for the future, you create it yourself.

HOW TO DEAL WITH UNRESOLVED QUESTIONS

One of the biggest global issues that we have had to confront over the last twenty years is climate change. Why are the polar caps melting? Is another ice age on its way? What's happened to the hole in the ozone layer? There are more theories about climate change than you have Facebook friends. Basically, there are two groups: the yay-sayers (global warming is real and it is man-made), and the nay-sayers (global warming is real but man's contribution is negligible). The yay-sayers are in the majority. The nay-sayers were given new impetus when, in 2009, correspondence between important climate researchers was leaked, and the public discovered that as little is known about the climate of the future as is known about life after death. But what should we do about climate change? Why do all climate summits fail? The teacher and author Greg Craven offers an interesting approach. His model does not center around the question of where global warming is heading or our role in the process; rather, he asks: should we be doing something about it?

The model illustrates a clever method for approaching any complex issue in a strategic way.

The following two questions form the starting point:

- Are we facing a man-made climate catastrophe?
- Should we do something about it?

Let's consider four possible scenarios:

1. We do something, but the global catastrophe proves to have been a false alarm. What would be the consequence?

We would have spent a lot of (taxpayers') money. Perhaps it would lead to an economic crisis, but perhaps we would also have created new markets through investments.

2. We do something, and the theory of a man-made global catastrophe proves to be true: we would certainly not talk about a "waste," rather about "salvation."

3. We do nothing, and there is no climate catastrophe. We would still have a lot of problems to deal with, but could breathe more easily with regards to the climate.

4. We do nothing, but the catastrophe comes to pass and proves to have been man-made: the world wouldn't exactly come to an end; at least some people would survive. But it would be an economic, political, social and environmental disaster.

Now compare the options "take action" (1 and 2) with "ignore" (3 and 4).

"Climate change is a global problem that cannot be solved by the global economy that we have, but only by a global government that we don't have." *Greg Craven*

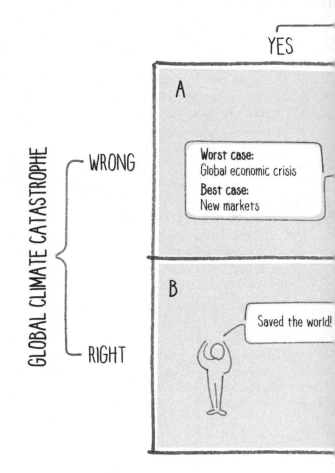

With this model, the teacher Greg Craven shows how necessary it is to do something about the climate catastrophe.

WHY THE SMALL FISH ARE OVERTAKING THE BIG FISH

"How can I make more money?" is a question all company managers ask themselves. One they don't ask themselves enough is: "Have I missed out on a new development?" So argues Harvard economist Clayton Christensen, who investigated why industry leaders usually miss the boat when it comes to developing groundbreaking innovations. His work is considered a milestone in economic research.

Christensen distinguishes between "sustainable innovation," the improvement of existing products that are designed to keep prices and margins high, and "disruptive innovation," the launching of new products that are typically simpler, faster and cheaper. In most cases, established companies try to improve successful products that already more than meet customer needs. Christensen calls it "overshooting": the managers of the company producing the product have no idea why their products are so popular and ignore what customers really want in favor of adding yet more nonessential features; for example, who ever uses all of the features in Microsoft Word?

Because these companies focus on their existing markets rather than developing new products, they don't see the threat of disruptive innovations coming from below. As a result, the overlooked disruptive innovation gains a share of the market and eventually ends up replacing the previously leading product.

"I don't know if it gets better if it's different. But it has to be different to be good." *Georg Christoph Lichtenberg*

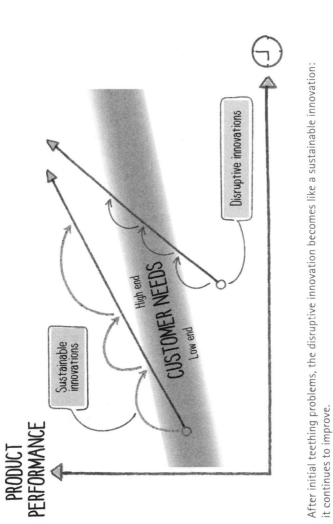

After initial teething problems, the disruptive innovation becomes like a sustainable innovation: it continues to improve.

WHICH INDUSTRIES STIMULATE THE ECONOMY?

According to the Russian economist Nikolai Kondratieff, the global economy develops in overlapping cycles or "long waves." At the start of each of these waves is a basic innovation, i.e., an innovation that causes a fundamental structural change and influences the whole of society. The new technology is invested in for forty to sixty years and thereby stimulates the economy—until the mode of production reaches its limits and there is no more growth. The search begins for a new innovation, which heralds the next cycle.

The first Kondratieff wave was triggered by the invention of the steam engine and the innovations in the textile industry. Steel and the invention of the railway marked the second Kondratieff. These first two cycles were dominated by Great Britain. The third Kondratieff—electrical engineering and the chemical industry—was dominated by Germany and America. During the fourth Kondratieff—the automotive and petrochemical industries—the USA established itself as a global power. It was the apex of industrial society. The oil crisis marked the changeover from an industrial to an information society: the fifth Kondratieff. With the global recession of 2001–2003, the sweeping potential of this technology declined. At the same time, the sixth cycle was being established: the health market, including biotechnology, the psychosocial sector (e.g., therapies), as well as environmental technology. Here's Leo A. Nefiodow, an expert on Kondratieff cycles, on the sixth cycle: "The health cycle isn't really about health care, it is just called this. More than 97 percent of the financial capital is spent on research into, and diagnosis, therapy and management of, diseases. It is in fact an illness cycle."

The length of the cycles, their triggers as well as their impact, are contentious. An important indicator for judging a Kondratieff cycle is the volume of work that it generates. In developing countries, no other industry is creating as many new jobs as the health sector.

"I think that nowadays it is health, not sex, that acts as a form of moral, i.e., social, control. It is all about controlling the body: staying slim, staying fit, eating properly." *Paul Strassberg*

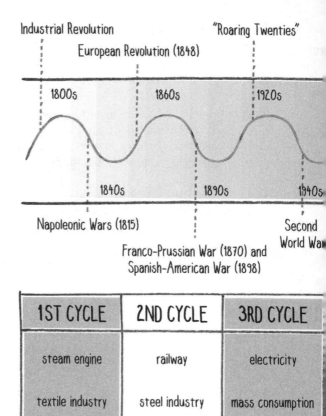

The decline of a cycle is exacerbated by conflict: e.g., the Napoleonic Wars, 1814/15, the Second World War (1939), the oil crisis (1973).

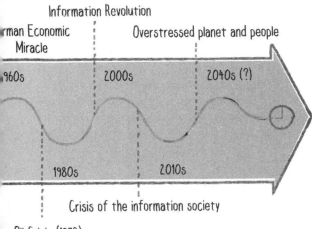

Information Revolution

rman Economic Miracle

Overstressed planet and people

960s   2000s   2040s (?)

1980s   2010s

Crisis of the information society

Oil Crisis (1973)

TH CYCLE	5TH CYCLE	6TH CYCLE
cars	information technology	biotechnology (?)
mobility	communication	health (?)
trochemicals industry	coltan (?)	DNA (?)

WHY COMPUTERS ARE OVERTAKING US

The answer can be found in the acronym CPU (Central Processing Unit). In 1965, Gordon Moore made a prognosis that still applies today: the number of transistors in a CPU doubles approximately every twenty-four months. In other words, computers become twice as fast every two years.

Let's look at the inner workings of a computer: imagine the main storage as a warehouse; it is the computer's long-term memory. The RAM (Random Access Memory) is the short-term memory. And the CPU is the processor that stores new and retrieves old data. The difficulty is not in storing more information—the warehouse can be enlarged as needed—but in processing it. The increased CPU performance means that we can now watch videos on our mobile phones when not so long ago we could only write text messages. Smartphones are supposed to be able to do everything at once—with the result that, just like PCs, they can crash. The technology experiences an information overload.

Moore's Law is not a law of nature. The most important question is: Is there a limit to a computer's performance? Yes, says Moore. No, says the futurist Ray Kurzweil: in 2049 you will be able to buy a computer for $1,000 with a processing power equivalent to the brain capacity of all living people. What does this mean? See the following model.

"I was surprised by its human abilities." *Garry Kasparov, after he lost against the chess computer Deep Blue in 1997*

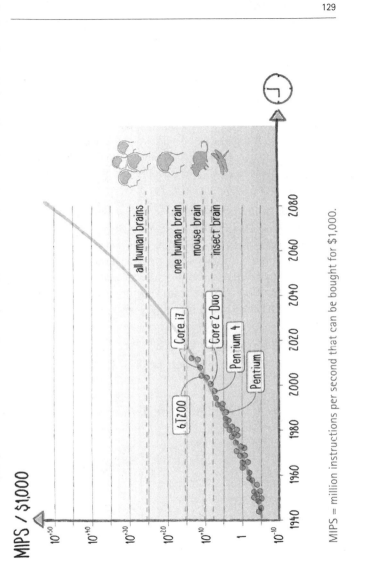

MIPS = million instructions per second that can be bought for $1,000.

WHAT "IT" IS

As we discovered with Moore's Law (p. 128), there are signs that computers could surpass the human brain and evolve into a kind of artificial intelligence. The point at which this will happen is called "technological singularity." Some people say it is the moment at which machines will gain the upper hand.

The more we use it, the more it learns. The more it learns, the more we use it. It is omnipresent. It is all around us. It imprisons our minds. It is supposed to distract us from the fact that we are trapped. It knows where we are. It knows where we were. It knows, more or less, what we are thinking. When it was created, it was not seen as intelligent. Because it is made up of codes and doesn't have a body, it is faceless. Because there are a million ways of accessing it, it is hard to say *where* it is. And because it is a combination of our intelligence and an alien digital memory, it is hard to say *what* it is.

It will change everything. It is hard to explain what *it* is, you have to experience it for yourself.

(Compiled from texts by Kevin Kelly, Ray Kurzweil, Eric Schmidt, Andy and Lana Wachowski.)

"It is what it is." *Erich Fried*

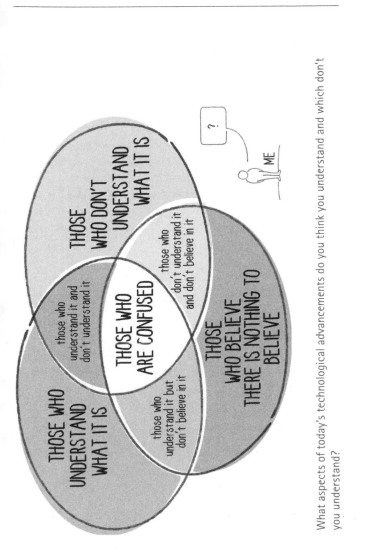

What aspects of today's technological advancements do you think you understand and which don't you understand?

WHY GENES RULE

Following the successful decoding of the human genome in 2001, molecular biology was raised to the status of a secular religion by many. And yet to date it cannot boast much success; cures for cancer and depression remain a utopian dream because the relationship between genes and the environment has proven to be more complicated than was initially assumed. And yet it is conceivable that in the future we will no longer turn to psychoanalysis or confession in our search for self-knowledge, but rather to the complete sequencing of our personal genome.

Possible consequences of increasing geneticization:

- **"Positive eugenics"**
  Prenatal and preimplantation diagnosis not only mean that genetic diseases will die out, they also prevent the existence of genetically "abnormal" people. (In Denmark, the number of Down syndrome babies being born has gone down by fifty percent since the introduction of screening throughout the country.)

- **"CSI" realities**
  DNA databases simplify the (worldwide) search for criminals.

- **New customer structure in health insurance**
  Classified according to customers' molecular makeup.

- **Personalized medication**
  Ingredients are chosen on the basis of a person's individual biochemistry.

- **New class society**

  U.S. molecular biologist Lee M. Silver (author of the controversial book *Remaking Eden*), predicts a division of society into "natural," "gene-enhanced" and "gene-rich" people. The "gene-rich"—about ten percent of the world's population—will no longer interbreed with the "naturals."

- **The end of solidarity**

  When social problems have their origins in a person's biological makeup, would the state and society no longer be responsible for social conditions?

- **Personal responsibility**

  The genome debate reveals a paradoxical simultaneity of determinism ("genes dictate your life") and personal responsibility ("those who have a predisposition for cancer are themselves responsible for trying to prevent it.")

- **Discovering an IQ gene**

  If such a gene could be found, asks sociologist Thomas Lemke, would not the notion of the inherent equality of all humans become obsolete, as there would no longer be a "natural foundation" for it? Would we abolish human rights? And above all: who would "we" be?

- **And also: finding the "missing link"**
  Through the hybridization of chimpanzee DNA with human DNA there would be a kind of rebirth of the Australopithecus, the first (pre)human.

"We are not equal to the perfection of our products. We are producing more than we can answer for. We also think we are allowed to do what we are doing." *Günther Anders*

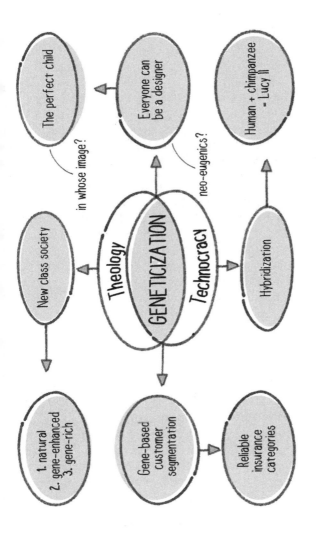

The model shows potential consequences of DNA encoding.

WHAT WE CAN BET ON

Humans have always tried to see into the future. Periods of crisis, in particular, fuel the desire for prognoses—although the prognoses in turn fuel the crises, because the (mostly) hostile future forces people to take action in the present. So in fact prognoses probably say less about the future and more about the present in which they are formulated.

One of the most interesting futures institutes is the Long Now Foundation in San Francisco. Cleverly combining a serious mission with a bit of fun, you can bet on the future at longbets.org. A few examples: by 2040 "Chi" will be recognized as a "life force" in traditional medicine; by 2060 there will be only three currencies worldwide; in 2100 it will be almost impossible to tell the difference between humans and machines. Anyone who bets has to explain the reasoning behind his or her bet, with the result that the site generally attracts real experts with sometimes abstruse but never absurd ideas.

Longbets is part of a large NGO which, with the help of patrons (including the Amazon founder Jeff Bezos), has set itself an ambitious task: to change our fast/cheap thinking into longer-term/better thinking. We shouldn't just be thinking as far as our next birthday or up to the next legislative period, but in longer time spans (compare: the "Sustainability Model," page 76). The project also confronts us with an uncomfortable question: do we really care what happens to the human race after we and our families are gone?

Kevin Kelly, cofounder of the initiative, has bet that by 2060 there will be fewer people on the earth than today. His rationale is that the trend toward small families with fewer than three children will spread to the "Third World." Is Kelly's prediction visionary—or deeply racist? His explanation implies that the rest of the world simply needs to adopt our small-family model and all the problems of over-population will be solved.

What is going on here exactly? While we are being encouraged to think about the future, we are also being given a platform to question precisely these prognoses. The negative bets on the site are also interesting: the last video store will close in 2015. The computer mouse will disappear in 2030. By 2035 the Aral Sea will no longer exist. By 2020 taxes will no longer be levied. Our favourite: in 2100 there will be no more racism.

"I prefer to remember the future." *Salvador Dalí*

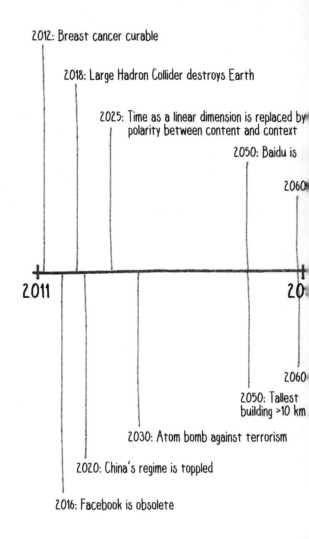

gger than Google

gital immigrants died out

2100: No more racism

2108: Companies run by artificial intelligence

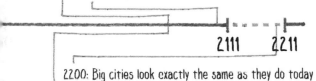

2111　　2211

2200: Big cities look exactly the same as they do today

2100: Global government

obal population < 2011

The model shows a selection of running bets on longbets.org.
What will you bet on?

HOW EVERYTHING WILL END

hasn't happened

MASS SUICIDE
For religious or other reasons,
many people commit suicide

MILLENNIUM BUG Y2K
Nothing happened

DOOMSDAY ARGUMENT
Playful mathematical
calculation according to
which humans will become
extinct by 2100.

MARS ATTACKS
Aliens attack Earth

MAYAN CALENDAR
The world will come to
an end on 12/23/2012

**EXTINCTION OF
SPERM CELLS**
Estimated: 2060

IMPROBABLE

DAYS OF WRATH
Biblical end of the world
according to Isaac Newton

**NUCLEAR
HOLOCAUST**
Global atomic war

GAMMA LIGHTNING
Earth becomes sterilized
by cosmic superexplosion

RAGNARÖK
Fight between gods
and giants will lead to
extinction

BIG CRUNCH
Universe shrinks to
size before Big Bang

An overview of apocalyptic scenarios.

ARTIAL DEMISE

GREENHOUSE EFFECT

ICE AGE
Earth freezes
(we are currently
in an interglacial age)

Earth boils, ocean
currents and
weather change
uncontrollably

PANDEMIC
Flus, viruses and epidemics
spread uncontrollably

CELESTIAL BODIES
Asteroids or meteorites
hit earth

SUPERVOLCANO
A series of earthquakes,
tsunamis and volcanic
winters make survival
difficult

**THE EXTINCTION
OF MEN**
Atrophy of the Y-chromosome

PROBABLE

ROBOT WAR
Computers will become
decision-makers,
see Singularity Model, p.130

DARWIN
The human species
will be evolutionarily
superseded

no more world

RED GIANT
The sun will swell up
and burn everything

no more life

BLACK HOLE
The earth will be swallowed up
or be completely transformed,
e.g., by CERN particle accelerator

SUN EXPLODES

OTAL DEMISE

APPENDIX

WHY CHANGE?

Change is generally welcomed or at least regarded as inevitable. But is this really so? Just as an example, why is a year in which a company earned the same as the year before regarded as unsuccessful? While searching for answers we came across this model by blogger Jessica Hagy.

The similarities between the way things are (A) and the way things will be (B) are often greater than expected (C). In other words: even following big changes, much stays the same.

But the model can also be read differently: Professor Philipp Zimbardo believes that there are three categories of people who can be defined according to which "time zone" they live in:

1. **Focused on the past:** "Past Negatives" (those who define themselves according to misfortunes and missed opportunities), and "Past Positives" (those who are nostalgic and romanticize the past).

2. **Focused on the present:** "Hedonists" (those searching for happiness) and "Nonplanners" (those who believe in fate, for whom the future cannot be planned, e.g., because of religion or class affiliation).

3. **Focused on the future:** "Planners" (life is what you make it) and "After-lifers" ("real" life begins only after the body has died)

In the Western world the vast majority of people are focused either on the past or the future.

So is C always getting smaller because we are too preoccupied with A or B?

"If it ain't broke, don't fix it." *Popular saying*

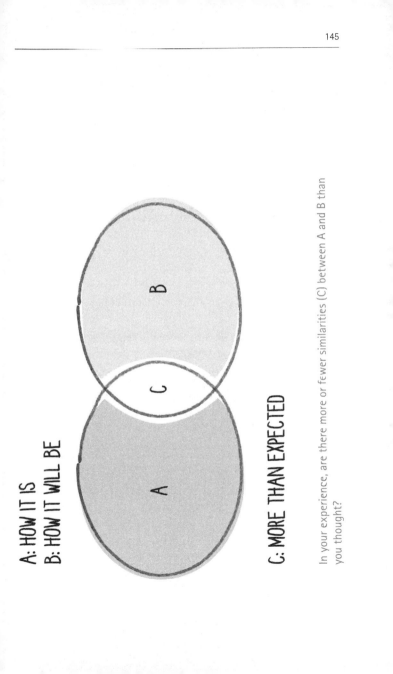

A: HOW IT IS
B: HOW IT WILL BE

C: MORE THAN EXPECTED

In your experience, are there more or fewer similarities (C) between A and B than you thought?

HOW TO EXPLAIN THE WORLD IN THREE STROKES

In visualizations, we distinguish between "divergent" and "convergent" images:

- **"Divergent"** means that an illustration depicts different approaches or options and this inspires creative thinking and offers new solutions.
- **"Convergent"** means that only the relevant aspects of a theory, approach or problem are depicted. These illustrations help us to understand complex ideas by radically condensing them.

On the following pages we will show you a few examples of how the world can be illustrated in a few strokes.

"The purpose of visualization is insight, not pictures."
Ben Shneiderman

1. **Triangle**

   How or why are A, B and C connected?

2. **Pie chart**

   What proportions of A and B make C?

3. **Circle diagram**

   A is followed by B is followed by C, then it starts again with A.

4. **Cause-and-effect chain**

   C results from B and B from A.

$$A \longrightarrow B \longrightarrow C$$

5. **Flowchart or family tree**

   Flowchart: If A, then B or C.
   Family tree: A results in B, and A results in C.

6. **Mind map**

From A, I think B and C.
From B, I think B1, B2, B3.

7. **Concentric circles**

A is part of B is part of C.

8. **Venn diagram (set diagram)**

Similarities between A and B, B
and C, C and A and A, B and C.

9. **Force-field analysis**

A contradicts B. C agrees with
B.

10. **Line chart**

The horizontal axis indicates
time (t), the vertical axis value
(A). B and C show progression
(bell curve, exponential curve,
hockey stick, etc.)

11. Two-dimensional axis model (Cartesian coordinates)

The A and the B axes have different parameters. The C curve shows a possible relationship between the two. Alternative: 4-field matrix. In this case, positions are shown instead of curves.

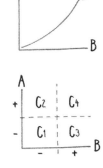

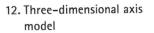

12. Three-dimensional axis model

A third parameter, the C axis, is added to the axes A and B. Different values can be entered in the coordinates system.

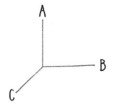

13. Pole model

The parameters oppose each other: black-white or right-left. Various positions can be represented.

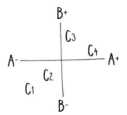

14. Radar chart or "spider"

Shows several parameters and their characteristics. Taken together, results in a distinctive shape. Good for comparisons.

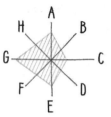

15. Table

For lists and combinations of A, B, C and D.

	A	B
C	AC	BC
D	AD	BD

16. Funnel

A and B and C make ... ?

17. Bridge

How do we get from A to C if B is an obstacle?

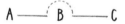

18. Iceberg

What forms the basis of A? What is visible? What is invisible?

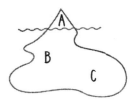

19. Pyramid

Who tells C what it has to do? Or how does A legitimize its position?

20. Tree

B and C grow out of A.

SOURCES AND PICTURE CREDITS

Anti-change Model
Philip Zimbardos' book *The Secret Powers of Time* as an animation by RSA: www.youtube.com/watch?v=A3oliH7BLmg
Image: by kind permission of Jessica Hagy, thisisindexed.com.

Back-of-the-Napkin Model
Dan Roam, *The Back of the Napkin: Solving Problems and Selling Ideas with Pictures* (Marshall Cavendish, 2009).
Information about low-cost carrier business (http://www.verkehrsjournal.at/cms.asp?editionId=12&articleId=56&action=artikel):
Image: own illustration.

Basic Income Model
A very good introduction to this topic can be found at http://www.citizensincome.org/
Image: own illustration.

Boom–Bust Model
George Soros, *The Crisis of Global Capitalism* (Little, Brown, 1998).
Image: ibid.

Braess Paradox
Linda Baker, "Removing Roads and Traffic Lights Speeds Urban Travel," in *Scientific American Magazine*, February 2009.
Wikipedia.
Image: own illustration based on various models.

Brand Model
Klaus M. Bernsau, "Semiotik der Marke—Ökonomie des Stils oder Stil der Ökonomie?" Lecture in Frankfurt an der Oder, 2005.
Image: with the kind permission of quietroom.co.uk.

Change Model
Jeff M. Hiatt, *The definition and history of change management*, www.change-management.com/tutorial-definition-history.htm, July 11, 2011.
Harald Welzer, "Was Sie sofort tun können: Zehn Empfehlungen," in *Frankfurter Allgemeine Zeitung*, December 30, 2010.
Image: own illustration.

Climate Disaster Model
An excellent introduction to the model can be found here: www.youtube.com/watch?v=zORv8wwiadQ
Image: own illustration based on G. Craven.

Corruption Model
The positioning of the countries in the corruption model is based roughly on the data from the Financial Secrecy Index FSI 2009, the Bribe Payers Index PBI 2008 (and partly 2006), and the Corruption Perceptions Index CPI 2010 (and partly 2008).
With the friendly support of Dr. Christian Humborg, Transparency International (www.transparency. de).
Image: own illustration.

Cosmogony Model
Wikipedia.
Image: own illustration.

Counterculture Model
Joseph Heath, Andrew Potter, *The Rebel Sell: How the Counterculture Became Consumer Culture* (Capstone, 2006).
Andrew Potter, *The Authenticity Hoax: Why the "Real" Things We Seek Don't Make Us Happy* (Harper Perennial, 2011).
Slavoj Žižek about cultural capitalism: http://www.youtube.com/watch?v=hpAMbpQ8J7g
Image: own illustration.

Decision Model
Kate Douglas, Dan Jones, "Top 10 ways to make better decisions," in *New Scientist*, May 2007.

Barry Schwartz, *The Paradox of Choice:* http://www.ted.com/talks/barry_schwartz_on_the_paradox_of_choice.html.
Image: own illustration.

Dictatorship Model
Based on an idea by the Facebook group TANK.
Image: own illustration.

Doomsday Model
Maarten Keulemans, *Exit Mundi— Die besten Weltuntergänge* (Deutscher Taschenbuch Verlag, Munich, 2010).
And good pointers from Ulrich Kühne.
Image: own illustration.

Dying Model
Elisabeth Kübler-Ross, *Interviews mit Sterbende* (Kreuz Verlag, Freiburg, 2005).
Image: own illustration based on various models.

End of History Model
Francis Fukuyama, *The End of History and the Last Man* (Penguin, 1993).
Andrew Potter, *The Authenticity Hoax: Why the "Real" Things We Seek Don't Make Us Happy* (Harper Perennial, 2011).
Image: own illustration.

Financial Crisis Model
Picture credit: we watched the documentary film *Inside Job* by Charles Ferguson, 2010, bit by bit and tried to illustrate and link together the most important elements in a flow chart.

Future Model
The "Arena for Accountable Predictions" can be found on the website www.longbets.org.
The full version of this text appeared in *Fluter* magazine, 87, 2010 ("Ich sehe was, was du nicht siehst").
Image: own illustration.

Geneticization Model
Ulrich Bröckling, Susanne Krasmann, Thomas Lemke (eds.), *Gouvernementalität der Gegenwart: Studien zur Ökonomisierung* (Suhrkamp, Frankfurt a.M., 2000).
Daniel Kraft, "Medicine's Future? There's an app for that": www.ted.com/talks/daniel_kraft_medicine_s_future.html.
Steven Pinker, "Personal Genomics—Or Maybe Not," in John Brockman, ed., *This Will Change Everything: Ideas That Will Shape the Future* (Harper Perennial, 2009).
Image: own illustration.

Globalization Model
David J. Smith, Shelagh Armstrong, *If the World Were a Village* (A & C Black Publishers Ltd, 2004).
Image: own illustration.

G-0 Model
David Bosshart's lecture: "Entgrenzte Macht-Spiele—Die Gewinner und Verlierer von morgen" ("Power games without boundaries—the winners and losers of tomorrow"), on March 16, 2011, at the Gottlieb Duttweiler Institute. Interview with Parag Khanna in December 2010.
Image: own illustration.

Innovation Model
Clayton M. Christensen, *The Innovator's Dilemma: The Revolutionary Book That Will Change the Way You Do Business* (Harper Business, 2011).
Image: own illustration.

Investment Model
Asle Finnseth, "Hva om Jesus var din finansrådgiver?," *Strek*, March 2008.
Image: own illustration based on Asle Finnseth/Adam Leonard Cable.

"Is the New" Model
Picture credit: developed by us, based on an idea by LeisureArts: http://thediagram.com/6_3/leisurearts.html.

Jumping-the-Shark Model
The "theory of cool" came about in a discussion between the authors and Jan Dirk Kemming and Mirko Derpmann.
Image: own illustration.

Kondratieff Cycle
Leo A. Nefiodow, *Der sechste Kondratieff: Wege zur Produktivität und Vollbeschäftigung im Zeitalter der Information. Die langen Wellen der Konjunktur und ihre Basisinnovation* (Rhein-Sieg Verlag, Sankt Augustin, 1999).
Image. own illustration based on various models.

Meaning of Life Model
Image: Detlef Gürtler, *GDI Impuls* 1, 2010.

Monogamy Model
E. Janssen, H. Vorst, P. Finn, J. Bancroft, "The Sexual Inhibition (SIS) and Sexual Excitation (SES) Scales: I. Measuring sexual inhibition and excitation proneness in men," in *Journal of Sex Research*, 39, 2002.
The "unfaithfulness survey," which determines how strong your brake and gas pedal are, can be filled out here: www.kinseyinstitute.org/research/sisses/index.html.
Image: own illustration.

Moore's Law
Wikipedia.
Picture credit: own illustration based on various templates.

Multitasking Model
Based on a discussion with the *New York Times* journalist Matt Richtel, author of the series of articles *Your Brain on Computers*: http://topics.nytimes.com/top/features/timestopics/series/your_brain_on_computers/index.html.
Image: own illustration.

Objectivity Model
Donna Haraway's scientific critique, *Simians, Cyborgs and Women: The Reinvention of Nature* (Free Association Books, 1991).

Othering Model
Stuart Hall, "The Spectacle of the Other," in M. Wetherell, S. Taylor, S.J. Yates (eds.), *Discourse, Theory and Practice: A Reader* (Sage Publications, 2001).
Image: own illustration.

Parenting Model
Judith Rich Harris, *The Nurture Assumption: Why Children Turn Out the Way They Do* (Bloomsbury, 1999).
Image: with kind permission of Judy Rich Harris.

Pioneer Model
Mark Wolverton, *The Depths of Space: The Story of the Pioneer Interplanetary Probes* (Joseph Henry Press, 2004).
Image: NASA.

Preemption Model
Catastrophe scenarios: Sven Opitz and Ute Tellmann, "Gegenwärtige Zukunft in Recht und Ökonomie," in: *Leviathan, Zeitschrift für Sozialwissenschaft*, 25, 2010.
Image: own illustration.

Prejudice Model
The idea of determining religious prejudices via a Google search and representing it in a diagram comes from the website www.reddit.com.

Quoting Authorities Model
Developed together with Mirko Derpmann.
Image: own illustration.

Religion Model
Based on discussions with Professor Mohn, University of Basle.
Image: own illustration.

Rhizome Model
Gilles Deleuze, Félix Guattari, *A Thousand Plateaus: Capitalism and Schizophrenia* (Continuum International Publishing Group Ltd., 2004).
Gabriel Kuhn, *Tier-Werden, Schwarz-Werden, Frau-Werden. Eine Einführung in die politische Philosophie des Poststrukturalismus* (Unrast, Münster, 2005).
Jim Powell, *Postmodernism for Beginners* (Writers and Readers, Inc., 1998).
Image: own illustration.

Science Model
Wikipedia.

Singularity Model
The quotes are taken from: John Brockman (ed.), *This Will Change Everything: Ideas That Will Shape the Future* (Harper Perennial, 2009) and www.die-matrix.net. The idea of technological singularity: Ray Kurzweil, *The Singularity Is Near: When Humans Transcend Biology* (Penguin Books, 2006).
Image: own illustration based on an idea on www.thecitrusreport.com

Sustainability Model
The text is a distillation of Christopher Peterka's essay "Give me Five": http://gannaca.com/blog/2011/05/give-me-five.
Image: own illustration.

Swarm Intelligence Model
Len Fisher, *The Perfect Swarm: The Science of Complexity in Everyday Life* (Basic Books, 2011).
Paul J. H. Schoemaker, George S. Day, "How to Make Sense of Weak Signals," in: *MIT Sloan Management Review*, Vol. 50, 2009.
Image: with the kind permission of Paul J. H. Schoemaker.

System of Government Model
Image: Detlef Gürtler.

3+1 Model
Max Tegmark, *On the Dimensionality of Spacetime*, http://space.mit.edu/home/tegmark/dimensions.pdf.
Image: The model was made available to us by kind permission of the author.

3-T model
Richard L. Florida, *The Rise of the Creative Class: And How It's Transforming Work, Leisure, Community and Everyday Life* (Basic Books, 2003).
Image: own illustration.

Transparency Model
Image: own illustration.

TV Series Model
Image: own illustration.

(Un)Happiness Model
Barbara Ehrenreich, *Brightsided: How Positive Thinking is Undermining America* (Picador, 2010).
Image: own illustration.

Web 2.0 Model
The impulse for this model came from David Bosshart's lecture "Boundless power games—the winners and losers of tomorrow" from March 16, 2011, at the GDI Institute, and a discussion with the author Teresa Bücker.
Image: own illustration.

THANKS

This book could not have been written without the generous help and support of many people. In particular we would like to thank our two coauthors: Detlef Gürtler (who wrote the System of Government Model, the Transparency Model, the Boom-Bust Model and the Meaning of Life Model, and who gave the book a focus in the early phases and inspired us with ideas right to the last); and Sven Opitz (for the Pre-emption Model). Invaluable support was given by our editor Laura Clemens and proofreader Ulrich Kühne.

We would also like to thank:

Aviv Agoor-Halevy (for critical feedback on the End of History Model and the G-0 Model), Fahim Alefi (for geostrategic advice on the G-0 Model), Elin Baustad (for her belief that there is always time for another project), Frank Baumann (for Arosa), John Brockman (for constant inspiration), Teresa Brücker (for perceptive insights into the world around us), Mirko Derpmann (for intelligent suggestions), Alain Egli (for input into the G-0 Model), Stephane Garelli, IMD Lausanne (for input into the G-0 Model), Jean-Marc Grand and Ulrich H. Moser from the GfM (for inspiring insights), Peter Haag (because he made everything possible), Daniel Häni (for the Basic Income Model), Judith Rich Harris (for parenting tips), Emil Holmer (for being a great neighbor), Dr. Christian Humborg (for the Corruption Model), Kevin Kelly (for a look into the future), Jan-Dirk Kemming (for heated and productive discussions), Parag Khanna (for input into the G-0 Model), Ketan Lakhani (for the initial idea for this book), Benno Maggi (for motivational feedback), Sita Mazumder, Women's Finance Conference (for a memorable occasion), Jürgen

Mohn (for the Religion Model), Christof Moser (for TANK), Dave Naef (for helping us on stage), Hanna Nilsson (for ongoing debates), Ola Nilsson (for challenging the G-0 model), Amy Novogratz, TED (for ideas), Jørgen Pedersen, University of Oslo (for questioning the G-0 Model), Christopher Peterka (for stimulating discussions and the Sustainability Model), Annette Ptassek, Deutsche Welthungerhilfe (for a memorable morning in Bonn), Matt Richtel (for input into the Multitasking Model), Ondine Riesen (for challenging discussions about values), Ohne Rolf (for visual and linguistic ideas), Paul Schoemaker (for the Swarm Intelligence Model), Franziska Schutzbach (without whom this book would never have been written), Patrick Tönz (for an insight into psychology), Andreas Wellnitz (for advice on images).

CONCLUDING REMARKS

The attempt to explain the world in models proved to be a much lengthier process than expected. Which theories have we forgotten? Which ones have we never heard about? How many have we misunderstood? Which ones have we overly trivialized through radical shortening? As in real life, some questions remain unanswered. However, we still hope that you had as much fun reading this book as we did writing it. If you notice any mistakes, if you want to criticize or add to particular models or suggest a new model, or if you simply want to make a comment, then write to us: mk@kasopilot.dk or rt@guzo.ch.

Models that didn't make it into the book are being continuously added to our website: www.2topmodels.com

If you enjoyed this book, you might also like our other two books, also published by W. W. Norton:

The Decision Book: Fifty Models for Strategic Thinking

The Question Book: What Makes You Tick?

THE AUTHORS AND ILLUSTRATORS

Mikael Krogerus was born in Stockholm in 1976. He is a journalist and writes for *Der Freitag*, the *Neue Zürcher Zeitung*, *Dummy Magazin* and other Swiss and German publications. He studied politics at the Freie Universität in Berlin, then at the Kaospilot School in Denmark. Krogerus is still not sure how to change the world.

Roman Tschäppeler, born in 1978 in Bern, is director of his company guzo, which develops and implements marketing and communications projects. He also works as a manager for a professional chef. He studied at the Kaospilot School in Denmark. Tschäppeler is working on a documentary film about Switzerland, gives lectures and is involved in the transformation of a local cultural center.

Philip Earnhart, born in 1965 in Switzerland, is a freelance art director. He has developed infographics and training material for Citi Group, Delta Airlines, DuPont and KPMG among others. He studied at the Art Institute of Seattle and lived with his family in Florida and Oregon. Since 2006 he has been back in Switzerland. He auctions artwork to finance wheelchairs for Jamaica.

Dag Grødal, born in 1974 in Bergen, Norway, visualizes change processes at Nordea, the biggest financial provider in the Nordic and Baltic region. He studied philosophy and ethics at Sogn og Fjordane College, then at the Kaospilot School in Denmark. Grødal is involved in a group that believes a solution to the conflict in the Middle East is possible: www.middleeastprogram.net

Jenny Piening is a freelance translator, editor and writer based in Berlin.

AV 5/16   1/15

EXPLAINING MY WORLD

EXPLAINING OUR WORLD